Table of Contents

Dedication

To my children, who are on their own personal journeys.

Throughout my life, I have made every effort to make the best decisions possible with the information I possessed at the time. I am proud of many of my choices; however, I must admit, there are others I am not. Overall, every decision I made helped shape the person I have become. After all, it will be your own choices that do the same for you.

I hope this book helps you better understand life's processes and the involuntary journey we all must undertake to become our best. These pages document a portion of my journey and the transformational processes I experienced. Although far from perfect, I am proud of the person I have become. My prayer is that at some point in your life you feel the same way about yourself.

When you are challenged by life's harsh realities, which at times you may, I hope you are encouraged by the insight acquired from these writings, and in some way, they help guide you through your crises. I will then rest, knowing my job as a father would be fulfilled by you doing so.

May the Lord always keep you safe, healthy, happy, and prosperous as He surrounds you with angels and holds you in His hand. I wish each of you the best of everything.

My love will always be with you.

Your father

Preface

Thank you for purchasing this collection of writings. Before you begin, please know that this body of work might not be everyone's cup of tea. In my previous career as a successful businessperson enjoying my version of the American Dream, reading this book may not have been my first choice. I had a lucrative career and a beautiful family. I was living at the right address, in the right neighborhood, and even drove the right cars; however, without warning, adversity struck and completely obliterated life as I knew it. I would have read anything that could have shown me a way out of my situation during that time.

Needing to understand what was happening to me, I was forced to assess every aspect of myself and answer questions I had never had to consider or think about before. However, the answers to these questions or solutions to my issues did not come immediately. For years, I was trapped in *perpetual torment* that mercilessly continued for what felt like centuries. These writings document what my soul felt as it cried out in unbearable pain while attempting to process fear, anger, and feelings of abandonment and depression. These writings, while at times are passionately intimate and, during others, wildly provocative, allow you, the reader, insight into the depths of the heartache and loneliness I felt while struggling to find solutions to end my adversity.

During that time, I vacillated in my relationship with God. In these writings, I share personal conversations and arguments I had with Him as I pleaded for relief which for a time did not come. In addition, I bore the enormous burden of guilt and disappointment for letting my family down. This book lays bare what unbridled emotions and a broken spirit sound and feel like under extreme pressure and without options. Finally, these writings represent a determination to survive, the earning of wisdom, confession, growth, and eventually, transformation and rebirth.

Through my journey, I share how the power of prayer, hope, belief in yourself and God allow incredible breakthroughs to occur.

Through the worst of struggle and adversity, I have found how one can still emerge victoriously by listening closely to God's voice, regardless of the situation. These writings express my discovery.

Please realize that I am not perfect, nor do I claim to be on any of these pages. I continually struggle with weaknesses and faults, just as anyone else; however, I understand that throughout life, we all will encounter situations and trials much more significant than ourselves. The incredible power, strength, and determination to succeed exist within us. When those traits align with the purpose God intends for us, divine success becomes inevitable.

So, whether you are currently facing a life challenge or not, yet choose to read further, I believe you will uncover lifelong lessons resulting in a deeper understanding of yourself. Additionally, I believe you will gain tremendous insight into building the inner drive necessary for strengthening your relationship with God. You will be poised to access all the benefits of His undying love and best for you.

I wish you the absolute best.

Steven LeMons

Introduction

L ife does not promise each day will bring us happiness, joy, or even abundant living. However, life does offer us opportunities. It provides opportunities filled with challenging and life-changing events that provide us with avenues for growth and becoming our best. By striving for higher standards and seizing our best life, we are all provided with events that place us squarely in the eye of a storm. Although we grow from such encounters, this tends to be the other side of life, the side no one wants to experience; however, at some point, most of us will. This opportunity, or other side of life, is often our catalyst for growth. It is adversity.

Webster's dictionary describes adversity as "a state or instance of serious or continued difficulty or misfortune." None of us can ever predict at what point adversity will happen, nor can we choose the method by which it operates. The truth is, as we continue living and experiencing life, everyone will eventually encounter coming face-to-face with it. Know that adversity usually shows up uninvited, on a mission, and with a specific agenda. It just appears, seemingly from nowhere, and when it does, you may find yourself feeling as though you're in the middle of a tornado with your entire life spinning out of control, meanwhile asking yourself, "How did I get here?"

The skies in your life that once were beautiful and blue now have suddenly and without warning changed. It appears all hell has broken loose, and nothing is the same. The good news is the events brought upon us by adversity require a re-evaluation of ourselves. We are now required to view our problems as opportunities for growth.

Unfortunately, adversity is simply a part of life's journey. As amazing as it is to have a happy and abundant life, I have come to realize that everyone, regardless of race, gender, level of education, or status on the food chain, at some point will encounter adversity. It is unavoidable. Adversity is the conduit for stretching, shaping, challenging, and humbling us. On the other hand, it forces us to progress and move forward into newer growth, maturity, and development phases.

Adversity can also be a mechanism for uncovering the true essence of our motives and those of others. It can expose relationships believed to be authentic when in fact, they rested on a foundation of dishonesty. Adversity supplies the pressure needed to move us beyond our comfort zone by providing the critical ingredients in our lives necessary for acquiring wisdom. Wisdom equips us with essential tools for managing change, excelling in life, and evolving into better decision-makers both during the event and throughout life. It is said that everything must change; this also includes each of us.

If life were void of adversity, many of us would never move or rise beyond our current state. Some would never come to know their true abilities or potential. In contrast, others would go through life either miserable or content to remain in a rut, just existing, doing the same things, never living, or never realizing their best selves. If adversity can be a catalyst for change, then change, although necessary, must happen for us to reach our true potential.

Unfortunately, adversity is simply part of life's journey. As amazing as it is to have a happy and abundant life, I have come to realize that everyone, regardless of race, gender, level of education, or status on the food chain, at some point will encounter adversity. It is unavoidable. We invite change into our lives by taking the initiative to step out on faith. In contrast, change involuntary forces its way into our lives during other times. Change then moves us beyond our place of safety and comfort. Life creates intersections or points where significant transition often occurs. A celebratory event such as graduation can simultaneously intersect with the loss of a job. Both are stressful, yet either event can be life-changing.

Relocating to another state and taking a new job, starting a new business venture, or even getting married, are all events or points where significant transition often occurs. Although viewed as positive milestones, these events can be highly stressful. On the other hand, we may encounter circumstances that do not cause celebration, and those often take our life in a direction we would rather refrain from exploring. For these events, it is only through continual refining and growth do we work through the adversity to move from a level of devastation and brokenness to one of wholeness and rebirth.

Webster's dictionary defines 'brokenness' as "being reduced to fragments, or reduced to submission." Through this submissive breaking, life offers us incredible opportunities for a richer and more profound sense of knowledge, self-awareness, and purpose. It is through this 'breaking' process wisdom is earned. However, if we ignore these events and minimize their significance, fail to accept the lessons they provide, or reject the opportunities they impart, we often risk repeating the same experiences.

In this book, what you will read occurred over eighteen years and under the weight and pressure of a broken spirit. Even though I considered myself a strong-minded well-rounded individual, there were times when I truly believed life as I knew it was over. At times, I sincerely believed death would have been a better option. Fortunately, die? I couldn't. I sometimes felt as if I had cried every tear out of my body.

I read, wrote, prayed, sought counsel, cried, screamed, got mad, cursed, got intoxicated, became sober, and rediscovered intoxication again, but to no avail. I still wanted to die, but for whatever reason, I just couldn't. Although my emotions ran the gamut, nothing changed until the adversity had run its course. Like a bad case of the flu, all I could do was try and feel better while plodding through the treacherous unknown that allowed nature to take its course. Whatever the lesson was, I definitely wanted to learn it, just to get this hellish situation over. In retrospect, I now realize that although my life seemed unbearable and in chaos, these experiences provided me with a richer and more profound sense of my purpose and myself. Through my self-centered rose-colored glasses, the experience gave me a greater understanding of compassion for others.

Through these experiences, I encountered a more defined mental, emotional, and spiritual perspective than before, one with a broader view that has elevated my life and spiritual awakening. This perspective has stretched my faith far beyond anything I could ever have imagined. I began to realize just how beneficial these lessons were to me, both then and now, including the invisible scars earned from them. Not only did I survive with a new lease on life, but I also thrived. If you're facing such calamities in your life, thriving and being happy can be a result for you too.

I have received blessings and benefits I never imagined thought possible. The truth is, I would never have volunteered for the unknown suffering and breaking brought upon through my adversity. I didn't choose it. I would never have. It chose me, and through it, I have found that true success belongs to those who have the faith, courage, and perseverance to face adversity head-on, look at it in the eyes, stand firm in the heat of battle, and walk away victorious. I can't say doing this is easy. I consistently failed because it wasn't that simple.

Although I survived, I cannot take all the credit for my success. I resisted, screamed, felt sorry for myself, got mad at the world, and even tried to run away from my circumstances. Ultimately, I had to stand and fight, which is what we all must do. However, like a battleship fresh from war, not only was

I forever changed by the events that happened, I still wear the invisible battle scars as proof of my engagement.

In addition to possessing the strength and courage to handle adversity, one must also have an intimate relationship with their God. This relationship goes beyond mere patronizing and pious surface prayers but must be one of deep commitment and communication. Adversity provides a needed purging and polishing in one's life, a letting go of the unnecessary, although oblivious baggage often carried with us. Whether it's the anger or resentment harbored for years against a sibling or relative or the arrogance or self-centeredness we flaunt in our day-to-day interactions with others, adversity levels the playing field.

As a result, refinement in the furnace of life produces humility, and it is through humility new perspectives originate. In the pages of this book, I am humbled to transparency and share my deepest and most intimate thoughts, prayers, and communication with God. These are my stories. Whether you approve of how I framed them or handled myself is not up to you. After all, they are my experiences. However, I pray that you read and receive your beneficial message.

As your spirit moves you, I pray that you are convicted with an open mind and find answers and hope for your situation or encounter. When the weight and pressure of a broken life bear down on your soul, where will your breaking point be? What will you do? Who will you become? For me, despite the good and not-so-good of my experience, I began to see life from an entirely different perspective, one that changed me emotionally, spiritually, and even physically. I hope that you are touched, encouraged, and moved to take action by these writings, and you encounter a deeper faith and hope for the best in your own life. For the Lord has made each of us and desires us to have a free and honest relationship with Him.

Although we may not be aware or convinced of it yet, God has a perfect plan and will for our lives, even while experiencing adversity. This collection of writings, poems, shorts, and prayers, represent some of the darkest and most agonizing periods in my life.

These are thoughts representing years of pain, torment, agony, and uncertainty. They are expressed through passionate emotion and transferred through the pen. My word choice is emotional, honest, and sometimes raw, but always truthful. They are words that come from the deepest parts of my soul.

My writings were inspired, resulting from the pressure and anxiety experienced through loss, anger, rejection, and ultimately, a soul destined to die through humility. Some came as a result of feeling as though I was being crucified, yet still, as stated before, I could not die even though I found myself dying multiple deaths in many ways.

Many of these writings found me broken, sweating in the dark of night, restless, and feeling like I was on the brink of insanity. I found myself crying and pouring my heart out to God, often begging for any degree of relief, comfort, or mercy I could find. Facing such calamities, I felt like a prisoner in a concentration camp under constant interrogation; one would do anything to make the brutal beatings, anxiety, and depression go away.

You may find these writings encouraging, many, provocative, or some maybe even offensive, but in them, I share the intimacy of my relationship with myself and Jesus Christ. Over time, my honesty with myself evolved. My honesty with God was brutal; why? Because there is nothing from Him that I can hide. Therefore, these writings represent the foundation of my transparency.

There was a time when I prided myself on supporting my family. I loved my job and what I did for a living. Growing up poor in a single-parent household, I yearned for more. My status and income provided me with the identity and credibility I craved. I was living a carbon copy of the American Dream. In my career, I was at the top of my game. For me, the solid but fragile pillars offered false substance; my career, credentials, my bank accounts, and relationships made me feel so bulletproof that I believed I could make anything happen at a moment's notice.

I was the guy who could always find a last-minute solution to the problem. If the bottom fell out of life, I could always step in and save the day like a superhero complete with black boots and a red cape. Whatever came my way, I was the six-figure fix-it man. However, nothing could ever prepare me for this adversity. Life took me down a path all its own. It presented me with a side of myself I didn't know existed, and so began the quiet yet powerful crucifixion (for lack of a better word) that would ultimately change my life and transform me into what resembled a resurrection. However, when hit with this side of reality, I could no longer pull rabbits out of my hats or leap tall buildings in a single bound.

It just didn't work anymore. In fact, nothing worked. I finally realized that this was something I could not fix, not anymore. My plans and actions yielded nothing because God had a different plan. During my lifetime, I have found myself at both ends of the spectrum, the high and low, and I am fortunate and humbled to share this small sampling of my life through these writings. I desire that regardless of your circumstances at the moment, you should always know that the Lord is good, His love is eternal, and that he is loving and merciful. He is a prayer or writing away. He has always been there for me, as He will be for you. In time, the Lord restored my life and filled it with purpose and power, which comes through spiritual confidence only He can provide. If you seek a purpose-driven life to achieve your goals and live your dreams to their fullest, these pages may inspire you.

I hope you enjoy reading this book.

"What you accomplish on the journey of life will determine your legacy. Wealth and riches may be temporal, but wisdom, patience, character, love, and the lessons learned while on your journey will last forever."

Steven LeMons

Part
I
Reality
A fall from grace

reality

Each of us is part of an incredible universe, one bigger than ourselves. It is a beautiful and fascinating place. It is a place of limitless energy that transcends time and space. We all have the opportunity to tap into the ancient wonders of its incredible power and tremendous energy, yet many of us never do. Some of us are unaware of its existence; therefore, we may never experience our true potential or happiness. We plod through life, often feeling defeated and not our best.

We constantly attempt to extract personal satisfaction from temporal novelties and trinkets sold to us on this earthly plane as the finite measure of happiness and success. In our competitive and capitalistic society, money becomes the 'adult scorecard,' and winning becomes the measurement of everything successful.

We sometimes allow our houses, cars, job, and status to drive our egos and define us. After all, I was one of those people. In reality, it is the intangible attributes that we often overlook. Wisdom, courage, persistence, compassion, and the like are traits we all should strive to achieve, although it is by other means they earn us the actual satisfaction and respect we crave. They build character and the overall enduring wealth we desire.

Being happy, experiencing true love, contentment, and joy is not a right but a privilege. These gifts are more significant than any pain, adversity, or adverse event which would seek to destroy them. Life can be wonderful and rewarding; however, we are the sum of all our choices. When we make choices that manifest in our favor, we pride ourselves on our actions.

In contrast, at other times, when making similar decisions and the results do not favor us, we can find ourselves depressed, imprisoned, and even ostracized by family and friends. When that happens, we can then find ourselves living a life filled with "what did I do wrongs, if-only-I-could-do-it-agains, and shameful regrets." Regardless of our challenges, appreciating life is the essence of living and the foundation of this book.

A beautiful dream can become a harsh reality at a moment's notice. One minute you are a starving actor or actress; waiting tables in some obscure little restaurant located at the end of nowhere, and in the blink of an eye, you could become a reality T.V. show superstar. You could be a corporate executive with a six-figure income, a beautiful home with a prestigious address, luxury cars in the driveway, an attractive, loving spouse, and two perfect kids, and in a few months, find yourself waiting in a food stamp line, wondering just how you got there.

In an instant, the high-life can suddenly become a painful and gritty low-life reality show, where you have the starring role. One phone call can immediately change your life. From nowhere, life has reared its ugly flip-side, and yours seem to be coming apart into a million pieces. Every pillar of false security you ever relied upon has been devastated. In no time at all, retirement funds and bank accounts become non-existent, marriage dissolved, good health evaporated, and the red Mercedes you were so proud of, right before your eyes, is being loaded onto the flatbed of a repo truck.

As single calamities, these challenges can wreak havoc on even the most faithful, but together, they can bring total devastation, leaving you feeling lost, confused, overwhelmed, and empty. Like a fully armed mercenary unit operating in stealth mode strikes with unrelenting blows and without mercy or compassion, your adversity attacks. Your formative foe is void of appearance, only actions.

Fairness has no place in its consciousness. Terror grips your soul. It is now your turn to experience the flip side of abundant life and be sucked into the painful whirlpool of adversity. Its ravages annihilate the comfortable and status quo. It dissects and exposes weaknesses in our lives that never would have surfaced had we not encountered the experience with laser focus. Adversity is and always will be a fact of life, just as success is to failure. It provides us with a sense of perspective continual success cannot. It engulfs us with purging and refining, which only this side of life can orchestrate.

The disruption of adversity challenges your confidence and spiritual beliefs to their core. You may find yourself repeatedly asking these questions, "Do I believe what I thought I did, or who I thought I was? Is there really a God?" Or, "Why am I going through this...why me?" You may ultimately come to think that your life is over. You may even begin to believe life is not fair or that only bad or unlucky things only happen to you; no one else could possibly be facing this but you. You have to be the only one.

As you tumble and freefall from the pedestal of privilege and freedom you once rested, while at the same time trying to grasp hold onto anything that could soften the blows of reality, you brace yourself for a hard landing. As you unsuccessfully attempt to process one event after another, when you least expect it, another blow lands squarely in the middle of your current turmoil. "Oh no, not cancer; he's never been sick a day in his life. No, not my child. Please take me instead but not my child."

"When I married, I did it forever. I never planned on getting a divorce." "How could you cheat on me after all we've been through together?" "Gay? What the hell are you saying? If you knew you were gay, why did you mess my life up by not telling me? Why did you lead me to believe you were straight when you knew you weren't?" "What do you mean, I'm fired. I've given my life to this company; this is all I know. How will I take care of my family?"

Suddenly, before you digest what is happening, life has taken you to a place you could never have imagined. Like a sailboat setting out on a cruise, no one in a million years could expect that in the blink of an eye, your boat would be in such deep, dark, uncharted, and turbulent waters. On the other hand, you feel as though you have been captured by a legion of mercenaries with special orders, not just to torment but ultimately take you out.

It is now when you must make unpleasant decisions, ones you never wish to think about, let alone decide. You try to find a reason, a rationale, some answer that satisfies what used to be your rational nature helps you to accept your current state of affairs, but you can't. There aren't any. While still in a state of denial, you find yourself facing reality so brutal, so unkind, and so unrelenting you would never wish such calamities upon your worst enemy—much less yourself. You constantly ask the question, "Why me?" As if the perfect answer will materialize and make it all better. "I'll just pinch myself and wake up," you say, but the nightmare is still alive and well, not just in what you see but also deep within the core of your being.

The invisible enemy is uncontrollably devastating everything in your life like a category five tornado that angrily intensifies as it unruly spins and gains strength. You think to yourself, "This must be a bad dream. Could this be a symptom from some misdirected morsel of food that didn't agree with me or something else?" The truth is, it's not.

Maybe if I take a nap and wake up from this maddening nightmare, everything will be okay. Life will go back to normal. After all, this kind of thing only happens to someone else, not me. What's worse is that you've just recovered from your last hit and finally get your arms around the previous adversity, when out of nowhere comes this seemly random Mike Tyson blow, just a month before your college graduation and degree. Here it comes, just after you've paid off your hospital bills and the car loan, is when the financial bottom falls out; It all seems so overwhelming!

In life, I have come to understand and appreciate the strength of the human spirit. Maturity, knowledge, and profound wisdom are earned through these experiences. However, as with acquiring all things of value, struggle and pain are part of their acquisition. It is unavoidable and required.

Everyone would like to possess the incredible benefits from having gone through the pain associated with this growth; however, there is a high price to pay for attaining them. To some, it's easier just to avoid the experience altogether. How will you react when life's flip side of life visits you?

"Sometimes things just happen. There is no rhyme or reason; it just does. It's not personal or sometimes even about you. It just happens to be your turn.
For everyone, it's not a matter of if; it's when. So, what will you do when the bottom does fall out of your life?"

Steven LeMons

"There is no growth without struggle. No success without failure. And no appreciation for life without first understanding the harsh reality that only life's experiences can teach us."

Steven LeMons

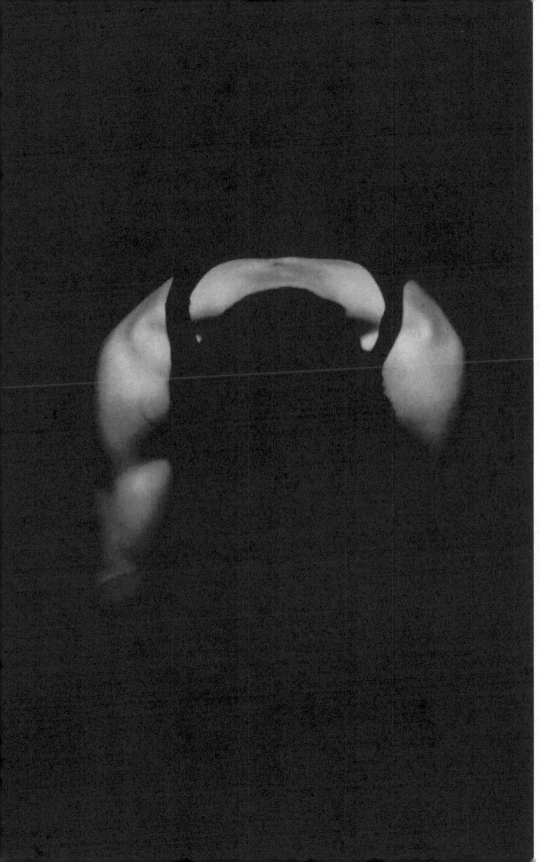

Introduction to
Fired

"As we go through life, as long as we work for someone else, many of us will run the risk or face the frustration and agony of being fired from a job."

R egardless of when or why it happens, it is hardly ever perceived as a positive experience. Whether presented to you as being let go, terminated, laid off, a job elimination, cut, being downsized, or just plain

fired, the result is always the same, devastating. Many of us may find ourselves placing so much stock in the company or our job security that our ego, status, or identity often finds itself interwoven into the fabric of the position we occupy. This writing, entitled Fired, reflects many of these thoughts. Fired represents a compilation of painful events and emotions I experienced being terminated during my career.

Having had full-time and part-time jobs, multiple assignments, appointments, and independent contracts, I have attempted to bring innovative ideas and set higher standards in my position and the workplace. Even more than my predecessors. In every role I occupied, an extreme effort was made to leave it in a better state than when I accepted it. When it comes down to it, whether fired or forced to resign, the aftermath and feelings associated with each event are usually the same.

However, over time, I realize God has always guided my path regardless of what direction my career has taken. I also believe that as you read these writings, you will come to know that He created me to be much more than just another employee.

Fired

"While taking that last walk, for some strange reason you always hear some song playing over the music system you recognize. A soft-rock Lionel Richie or Billy Ocean song from the eighties that catches your attention; but what's funny is that you'll hear that same song for years; long after you've left the building.

I was fired today. For what reason, I don't know. However, at the same time, maybe something inside me knows already.

Getting fired is not a pleasant experience, regardless of what form it takes. Whether you've been laid off, riffed, or phased out, it can be devastating no matter what label the organization uses as an excuse.

At its root, getting fired is about being rejected, shattering a person's self-confidence. The truth is, whether you are an employee who struggles in the course of their duties or someone who is considered a stellar performer when it comes to being fired, everyone will handle the situation differently. It usually isn't the best of feelings.

For most employees, a firing event usually lies in wait. It eventually sneaks up on you when you least expect it, ambushing your spirit, soul, and of course, your finances. It can leave you shattered in a million pieces, break you mentally, emotionally, physically, and again, financially. Sometimes all at once.

In fact, you may be entirely clueless about the incoming firing until you find yourself called into what appears to be a routine meeting, only to find the players in attendance not be the usual suspects. It is then when you discover the HR manager in attendance is not there to have a warm cup of coffee but to give you your final farewells. During this time, you realize that you've just begun the process of taking the initial steps of a long walk to the human resources gas chamber. When I walked into that office, I knew I wasn't heading toward good news.

When I was fired, they wanted to see a reaction, an outburst, or a man out of control. They were really curious to see how I would go out; how I would take it. Would I just leave and go quietly, or would I act like the Tasmanian Devil from the Bugs Bunny cartoon on steroids? Or, as my grandmother would say, "Like a combo fool?" My instincts told me something was about to happen, go down, take place. Interestingly, when the two people in charge of this event called me into the office, they had already taken the necessary precautions to protect themselves – just in case the scales tipped, and I decided to go postal.

In this instance, both the boss and his henchman came to my office and stood by the door. "Hey, buddy, you got a minute?" "Sure," I said. "Let's go over to my office and talk," said the boss. Well, to me, this wasn't too unusual. The idea of going to his office to have a conversation had taken place countless times. Why would I expect anything different today? The fact is that each day stands on its own. That's the beauty of life. As Forrest Gump's mother always said, "Life is like a box of chocolates; you never know just what you're gonna get."

On this particular day, that statement was never more accurate. As we took that walk to his office, I felt this time it was slightly different. It was more like they were escorting me rather than walking with me. Oh, oh, by that time, my inner alarm had started to go off. My thoughts recalled the robot in the old "Lost In Space" television series. "Warning, Warning, danger Steven LeMons, danger, danger," the inner me shouted.

For whatever reason, something didn't feel right. Perhaps it was my instinct warning me about the chaos about to ensue. As we entered the office and sat down, the boss' mouth began to move, sort of like in slow motion. He spewed out sounds similar to those of the teacher in the Charlie Brown television show, wah, wah, wah, wah, wah, wah, wah. Finally, the strategic words he had so finely crafted landed on my psyche like napalm falling through the jungles of Vietnam in the '60s. Boom, boom, boom, each one hitting its designated target. After all, why shouldn't the words hit their target with impact? It's a firing, not a coaching session. The first one hit my ego, the second attempted to break my spirit, and the third tried to devastate my soul.

"Hey Buddy, we're going to have to make some changes; this isn't working out; we're going to have to let you go." Straight to the point, complete, done, and dusted.

There it was. It was the bomb you were not anticipating on this day, but you got it as an unwelcomed bonus. The sleeper bomb that once dropped left the room in total silence. Although the quiet was probably only a few seconds, it felt like a half-hour. In sales, there is an expression that states, "The first one who speaks loses." The fact is, no one spoke. There was dead silence. The truth is that when something like this happens to you, it's difficult to process instantaneously.

Your mind is whirling as you attempt to find the right words to say. All the while, there is this sinking feeling where the information has to filter down through the layers of your self-confidence, integrity, and what you perceived to be a job well-done. A part of you is wondering whether this is a bad joke or reality. But by the time you awake from your mini stupor, you realize it's the real deal.

We all know that life teaches us a thing or two about words. After all, a firing is about the words first and the aftermath later. So now that this little episode had happened and there was a gaping crater in my soul the size of Lake Superior, I couldn't help but replay those words repeatedly in my head. So, let's just break these words down to understand better. First of all, "Buddy" is not my name. Buddy LeMons doesn't have a very nice ring to it. So how did it get from Steven to Buddy? Was Buddy an imaginary person to target the arrow of doom instead of addressing me by my name?

When I was growing up in the days of black and white television, there were only three networks; Buddy was an affectionate name given to a dog or puppy on one of those Leave It To Beaver—Father Knows Best type television programs. "Come on, Buddy," "Go fetch, Buddy," said the little blond-headed kid in the blue jean overalls. Buddy is also another term for a pal or friend. "Oh, that's just my buddy; he's my pal." In this instance, the question is, are we friends or pals, or just good buddies? I don't think so. You don't fire your buddies, do you? The name Buddy just didn't fit this particular situation.

Next, "We're going to have to"…what is this 'we're' thing? Who is 'we're?' Actually, we're, is a contraction for 'we are.' So, if you are the person in charge, the owner, the person where the buck stops, the boss, the big cheese, then who is 'we are,' or the 'we're's'? Where did they come from? I suspect this event has been preplanned, prepackaged, sliced & diced, and discussed with others who you, the boss, have already convinced that firing me is a great idea. Pretending like we were still on the same team was to soften the blow. It did not work, and I could see right through the act.

My question is that if you're the boss, and you sign everyone's paycheck, who, with any backbone or marginal degree of sense, is going to disagree with you? You could fire your mother, cheat her out of her paycheck, deny her unemployment, and no one would say a word—only agree. "You're right, boss. She needs to go." So again, I'd like to know, who are these invisible's, known as we're's, that are in on letting me go? Next, "This isn't working out." What does that mean?

My question is, "What is it that isn't working out?" The company hired me to uncover the root causes of the business's problems. Look under every rock, nook, and cranny of the process. I did that and found them. That means that I did a good job, right? The truth is, you didn't want those root causes to surface for fear of being implicated, so to protect yourself, you were thinking that you'd better let me go before the higher-ups know what's going on, or rather, what you're doing.

Another little critical tidbit you'll sweep under the rug is that I uncovered how you were abusing and stealing from the very people you were entrusted to protect: your employees. I also discovered you were falsely manipulating information and passing it onto your bosses because it made you look good, at least on paper. Go figure. However, when I brought the root causes behind the issues to your attention, you acted as if you knew nothing about them, even though you, the puppet master, endorsed all the activities. That probably had something to do with your firing me, right, your lack of integrity?

And what was it about this "not working out" that wasn't working out? All you had to do was do the right thing, and it would have all worked out fine. But it didn't, and it wasn't, because, in your attempt to hide the truth from your superiors, you would rather bury your "ill-gotten" gains than have them find out what you were doing. After all, that's why I was hired in the first place, to uncover root causes, right?

What I represented to you was your link to being exposed. However, it was never my intention or motivation to expose you. I had no incentive. My only incentive was to help find solutions to problems and work with you to make those solutions a reality, not take the information and use it against you. It was your insecurity that led to that belief. You had to protect yourself, right? And finally, the last part of your statement was, "we're going to have to let you go."

The question I had was, "let me go where?" Where is it that I am to be let go to? Are you going to load me into a car blindfolded, take me out on a long dark stretch of highway, drop me off on the side of the road, dare me not to take off my blindfold for five minutes, and wander through a deep dark forest in search of a way back to civilization? Since I'm bad with directions, you know I'd have a hell of a time getting out of the woods and finding my way back home.

Anyone who has ever had these statements made to them already knows what they mean, even though they do not have specific clarity. They are stock phrases that are only a formality. "We're going to have to let you go" really means you're fired; however, by saying, 'We're going to have to let you go" insulates the person making the statement because it softens the words. Oh, and by the way, there's that "we're" again. In reality, we still have not clarified who precisely the 'we're's' are yet.

Let me think. Do 'we're's' belong to the 'Invisible Society of "We're,' Local #666? Or are the "we're's" that close-knit posse that will do anything to survive within a dysfunctional work environment even if it means playing the Judas role, lying, or agreeing with the boss to get their needs met? Or is it that group who will throw anyone under the bus, drive over them, and back it up for a second pass just for a small ego-stroking bone thrown by the boss?

Are they the ones who laugh at the boss' jokes even if they aren't funny? Say "bless you" right on cue after every sneeze, or openly align themselves in false support of your efforts while behind your back, cut you to shreds? Could this be the "we're's" you are referring to?" Regardless, your boss and the "we're's" have all gotten together to let me go. So, where's the big send-off from Local #666? Why is it that only the two of you showed up? I guess no one else got the invitation, right?

Back to reality, my heart sank after my soon-to-be ex-boss spoke those cataclysmic words to me. I felt empty, dizzy, and felt as if I were in total shock and wanted to throw up. Come to think of it, I did want to, but I couldn't let them see me weak.

My mind raced, and in a single nanosecond, darted from one thing to another and from person to person. Thanks to my efforts, employee productivity, profits, and morale were all up. Finances were clean, customer satisfaction, and employee retention, all up. I was a golden employee. Then pow! Wake up call, reality check. Come down from the ether, Steven! Regardless of my current feelings, I couldn't put up a verbal fight once I heard and processed those words. In fact, all the fight had drained out of me.

When the words "you're fired" are directed at you, your mind may know everything it would like to say, but the words just do not

43

come out right. And when they do, they usually don't make sense. Not only do they sound like gibberish, but they also get spun around, twisted, and blown into oblivion by the opposition. Remember, they've already planned and rehearsed this entire event. The decision has already been made. What's more, is they've fortified themselves to overcome your objections. So, whatever comes from your mouth, they already have a pre-rehearsed script in place to shut you down.

After a few stabs at nothingness, there's not anything else you can do. Nothing! That's when you realize it's over. Your confidence and pride are about to be packed into an ugly cardboard box that previously contained automobile parts or copy paper you picked out of the trash. So, what do you do now?

Something inside you really wants to go ballistic, to tell someone off, let everyone know how hurt you are so your allies can see the inequity of the act. But you don't. Instead, you leave. You're done; it's over. So as normal as you can act, you get up, walk back to your office, gather your things, put them in that old box, and prepare to leave. You don't want to see or talk to anyone during this time. You just want to leave the place forever and never look back.

You have been banished to the gulag of unemployment. Rejected by the boss, the work cartel, the posse, and by the 'we're's', and that's it. As you grab your auto parts box and take that pallbearer-induced robotic walk to your car, many feelings swirl about you and saturate your being. You feel used, hurt, angry, frustrated, embarrassed, yet at the same time, you feel liberated. You have no clue what you've been released from or what's next, but a burden has been lifted from your shoulders.

It never fails that as you take that slow walk through the facility, for some reason, you always hear some eighties Lionel Richie or Billy Ocean tune you recognize playing over the sound system. Passing co-workers in the

hallway on your way back to your office, you ask yourself the question, "I wonder whether she knows. Is she one of the 'we're's'? There's Dave; I wonder if he had anything to do with this? He never liked me anyway. Could he belong to Local #666?"

Stepping outside into the beautifully bright and sunny day, the most pressing question on my mind at this time is not why I was fired, but what next? What will I do next? What do I tell my wife? What will she say, and how will she take it? Oh, and speaking of a Tasmanian Devil, my wife could turn into one because I was fired again. I know this for a fact. I do hate to disappoint her, but I often wonder why these types of things keep happening to me?

Why can't I see wrong and just look the other way? Why just keep working and getting paid like everyone else? Why must I always be the one to call out the bad behavior? Maybe it's not too late to get an official application and join the "we're's," but hell, I still probably couldn't keep my mouth shut in the #666. My life is filled with many 'what's and why's.' I was hired and paid to make assessments, find problems, initiate productivity, and create solutions. I did that, yet once I completed my job, I was left without a job because the issues uncovered and faults accompanying them came right back to the man who hired me to fix them in the first place. When the corporation suggested he hire me to find the problems, in his mind, he never thought I would ever uncover them, but I did. Finding the root causes only placed him in a position where he had to ask himself, "Now that this man has uncovered the truth, what should I do with him?" To him, the answer was obvious. Although I loved every minute of the chase, it is still an odd job to have.

As I reached the safety and comfort of my car, I closed the door and finally felt relieved. It's over. It's as if I have left a concentration camp. I now see and hear the cries of the prisoners dragging the chains and shackles that bind their every move. This experience has exposed what should be apparent, yet many trapped failed to see. It shows the power and fear Pharaoh and his soldiers wield over the minds of his employee's income and even their families. I wanted to help make the situation better for everyone in some small way. But I was fired. Maybe through some strange play of fate, I even fired myself. Working there allowed me to grow mentally, physically, emotionally, and spiritually.

Although this could devastate me financially, I would like to know if I have learned the lesson God sent me there to learn; or will I repeat the same experience over again in another quasi-concentration camp? I hope not, because it is a high price to pay for such a lesson. I now know that life is not always about a job or paycheck. It is not about saying 'bless you' just to be included or part of the "we're's." Life is about having a purpose and walking in divine will, whatever that may be for you. Being what God would have me to be and standing firm in the midst of chaos, betrayal, and backstabbing, regardless of what the environment looks like around me. My sufferings allowed me to know that in my way, I prevailed.

I now know that people will stay in a hellish situation, even if it causes great pain and breaks their spirit. Why? Because of fear and not possessing the courage to leave. It becomes easier to adapt to their environment than explore successful options that could help them overcome their fear. Whether it be a job, an abusive relationship, or any other life-draining situation, many would rather die than escape, be killed instead of trying to get out and complain rather than change. I thank God I am not one of those people.

*"On the journey of life
you will meet many individuals.
Some are moving forward,
some stand still, while others
are unaware they
are not moving at all.
Life and time always move forward.
Keep moving with it"*

Steven LeMons

Scared

"You don't matter anyway."

Have you ever been scared? Have you ever been so terrified that it seemed as if destruction and death were imminent? Not just frightened, but so terrified of the calamity upon you that you couldn't eat, sleep, or think of what to do to remedy your situation? I have.

Fear and its demonic stench tried to break me, making me do things that I would never do under normal circumstances just to avoid facing it. I was too scared to quit, yet equally too terrified to continue living that hell. Through its perverted and endless attempts, Fear eventually found a way to get inside my head, bullying, intimidating, and creating so much confusion that it stole my confidence, self-esteem, and what small shred of joy I possessed. I did not know which way was up.

Fear emasculated me; like human road-kill ran over and left for dead. I was nothing more than human garbage to the enemy: just another conquest, another spiritual statistic with a broken heart now suffering defeat.

Fear became so real to me that I could feel it. It had a face, a look, even a smell. It possessed a power, even a voice so sinister and convincing until the tone of its words led me to believe something tragic was going to happen at any given moment, even though the possibility of such an event was remote.

Fear created such a dreadful illusion until it prompted me to believe a negative outcome was inevitable. I was convinced my life was over. Its infinite power and devastating tentacles of lies wrapped themselves around my mind, persuading and intimidating me into believing there was absolutely no way out of my horrid situation. All the while, the sinister voice kept whispering, "Why not just go ahead and do it, end it all? Your family and everyone else will be better off without you. You don't matter anyway. You're a has-been and a failure. You're never going to get out of this."

I tried to outrun it, outthink it, and outlast the fiery darts thrown at me from hell, only to discover my problem became more compounded when I bought into the lie. My attempts at rationalizing and understanding just how I arrived at this place were all in vain. "Did I spend too much money? Did I think too highly of myself? Was I irresponsible? What could I have done differently to change this outcome? What sin could 1 have committed so awful that it justifies this?

A million questions swirled about my head, yet I could find no rational answer to satisfy my anxiety and dysfunction. My circumstances called for me to reach deep within my most secret places and take action. Believe me; I wanted to. I tried, but I just couldn't. I froze. There were just too many obstacles weighing me down.

Hellions attacked me from all directions, not one at a time, but sometimes all at once. It was the loss of my job, the repossession of my car, multiple business failures, a broken marriage, an illness, taxes, pride, guilt, loss, and life itself, all happening at once. I found myself petrified, weighed down like an overworked slave. I felt the heavy bags of life strapped to my back like a beast of burden becoming weaker with every step I took. Like a prizefighter in the fifteenth round, fear had me against the ropes, my head bleeding profusely, both eyes almost swollen shut. I felt my lip cut in multiple places, and my legs felt like rubber. Blinded by the streams of blood flowing from the open gashes on my forehead, I was overcome by the thought of what the outcome might be. I wanted someone, anyone, to ring the bell so that I could give up.

I was done, and through the worst of my experience, I still held onto a tiny yet determined shred of hope and belief. The hope that one day this would all be over, and the belief that regardless of what the current situation appeared to be, God was still in control. I held onto the belief that I was just one step or one phone call away from greatness, while at the same time, I found myself battling the foul play of demons, hell-bent on making sure I was two steps closer to total devastation. For every step I took forward, I seemed to be taking two more backward. Oh my God. Oh my God! My soul cried out in pain.

Then, amidst this hell, God spoke to me through my spirit. He said, "This current state is necessary for you to become the person I've predestined you to become." I have come to recognize that my weakness and fragility of faith is human despite my spiritual belief in You and Your word. All this so-called armor You have provided me with through Your word I know exists, yet I am still terrified.

I don't know how and I don't know why. I don't know what, nor do I know when this all will end, but I do know that You are stronger and more powerful than me, and You have to be in control. Lord, I know You hear my cries. I know You understand my heart, pain, sorrow, and You know my destiny. Although I am weak, I am also strong, for I know within the depths of my soul that You know what is best for my life, not only for me but for those I love. I realize that I was created to succeed, not to fail, and with every failure, the experience is a building block dedicated to the foundation of my growth and development.

I know that I cannot just lie down, give up, or die. I must fight! I was not built to fail. You did not create me for failure, but one who learns from failing and succeeds. I believe nothing can separate me from your love, not circumstances, adversity, fear, defeat, or anything that will ever keep me from my strength which lies in You. Although my spirit and soul embrace these fundamental truths, my mind and body are no longer willing participants. For in life, it is about the process. It is the process of 'becoming' that is so difficult. It is the process brought about through adversity where wisdom is earned, and fears are slain. I have heard it said that "Everyone wants to go to heaven, but no one is willing to die."

Maybe I am one of those people. Perhaps I am not. On the one hand, I believe myself to be invincible through faith, yet on the other, I find myself unequally matched and powerless against this foe. Yes, I am terrified. I am currently facing fear, an enemy I do not ever wish to encounter again in this lifetime. But I realize that being a child of the living God; I will face him again and again.

Do I get angry at what You are doing to and with me? Yes. Do I think life is unfair and sucks? Sometimes. But if there is truth in the Bible, I have to believe that everything happens for a reason. Oh God, deliver me. My soul cries out to you. I am terrified. Deliver me. Amen.

At What Point Do I Give Up?

Today, they repossessed my car. I was **three months** behind on the payments. **Tomorrow**, my lights are to be disconnected. The water bill is **due,** and I cannot pay it. My house goes into **foreclosure** in less than ten days. There is nothing in the cupboard to **eat**. My bank account is overdrawn; there are **no savings,** 401K, investments, rental property, **health insurance,** CDs, or anything left. **No income**. Nothing. **Everything is gone**. There are two **children**, a wife, desolation, and me. There is **nothing left** but a prayer in search of a **miracle**. After everything has been exhausted, at what point do **I give up on God?**

"Give me back what the locust has destroyed. For I may not be worthy of your mercy, grace, or favor, yet I still desire and claim it done. I see it done. I believe it done."

Steven LeMons

THE STRENGTH TO WRITE

Lord, with all my strength, I am trying to hold onto what is left of my screwed-up life. I may not know just what to do or how to do it, but I continue doing what I know, and that is to write.

This adversity has pulverized me. I found myself broken down to what I thought was my least common denominator, yet I fought and clawed my way back with every ounce of strength I had to gain a shred of dignity and self-respect. At some point, I began to realize it was only my ego and pride I was struggling to feed.

When coming face-to-face with the ugliness of overwhelming adversity and the nastiness of being broken, there are times each of us turns to our vices to fill a vacuum or ease the pain. The problem I encountered in doing so was I wished I could have tiptoed through the tulips of life to find the perfect anesthesia for softening the relentless blows I was experiencing, but I couldn't. There was nothing that could fill my void.

Everything I tried left me feeling even less fulfilled and defeated than before. In life, whatever your poison is, whether alcohol, drugs, sex, porn, anger, withdrawal from the world, gambling, or violence, when you become overwhelmed by the sensations of the process, we often look for something, anything that presents us with a different sensation from what we are currently feeling. We seek almost anything that provides an escape, an out, or a crutch that helps us cope, even if it's temporary.

For me, aside from what became time-wasting pursuits at anesthetizing myself and walking away with a hangover, I found a productive escape through journaling. Writing helped me maintain my sanity and sense of perspective in the midst of experiencing dismal times. While navigating this phase of my life, writing became my refuge. It was a way of expressing myself without explaining to others or incurring unnecessary judgment. When I was without true friends, I wrote; when I ran out of people to talk to or when they refused to listen anymore; I wrote. I wrote when I didn't have money, hope, or couldn't pray anymore yet still desired to express my thoughts to God.

In writing, there is no embarrassment, judgment, or condemnation. It is just the pen, paper, or computer and your thoughts. Although writing could not satisfy all my desires or eliminate the pain, nothing enabled me to express the genuine emotion, joy, or heartbreak of each moment like putting pen to paper did.

Lord, you have brought me through many trials, as well as the anger and disappointment associated with failure. You are with me through brokenness and many of my bleakest days— days I didn't think I could get through. You've helped me manage emotions I felt ill-equipped to handle, and you allowed me to write. You have built me up, been my refuge, my hope, my manna, and my strength. Through difficult times, you have guided me. You have spared me through your gifts of grace and mercy, and you have always supplied my daily bread.

You have blessed me with talent, gifts, and the ability to generate income. You have blessed me with good health, skills, favor, and experiences that have empowered and enabled me to grow. You have educated me, trained me, motivated and inspired me. You have even wrapped me in the warmth of your love only to disassemble me again and put me back together better than before. And through each of these experiences, I still find it hard to hold on. Each day I feel myself losing my grip. I get weaker day by day and find it harder to hold on. But now what? I am torn by these mixed messages, and I desire you to make them more transparent. What do you want me to do?

Although I currently struggle to see life from a clearer perspective, I visualize a new life outcome more beautiful and alive than ever before. How do I capture it? What steps should I take to make it truly mine? How can you ask me to jump into the sea in the middle of a storm when you know I cannot swim? Why would your assignment require me to give of myself in ways I do not believe possible—to those I would never have had the opportunity to encounter? How? Why? What?

I have come to write to the glory of God! Even when I am hurting. I write when I do not feel like I can go on or when my faith is weak. For me, writing is my prayer. It is my confession. It is the voice of my spirit on paper. Writing provides me a way of keeping my perspective and sanity; whether critics see my work as good or not, I still write. Do I get angry at what you are doing to and with me? Yes. Do I think life sucks and is sometimes unfair? You bet I do. But if the Bible holds true, I must believe that everything happens for a reason. In my experience, I have found that the sling blade of life swings both ways. There are times when it turns in your favor, while during others, it may not. Only your perception of the situation and what you choose to do about it makes the difference.

Lord God, I am gifted, talented, and powerful. You have made me for your reason and divine purpose. Raise me. Exalt me, oh Lord, restore, replenish, replace, renew, reorganize, reinvent, and revitalize my spirit. Please give me back what the locust has destroyed. Please allow me to craft words that express myself through writing continually? Let me glorify you through the voice of my hand.

Give me the strength to hold on until you change my situation, not in fear, but through your holy spirit and in your undying strength? Even if I am not worthy of your favor, I still ask for it and claim it. I see it done. I believe it is done. In Jesus' name, I pray. Amen.

The Lone Star Card

There was nothing in the pantry or refrigerator to eat. I was without any money or available resources to get anything. Even if I could, I had no way or means to pay anyone back. There were two hungry kids, and there wasn't anything left in the house but exhaustion.

Getting emergency food stamps was our last resort. After what felt like a humbling and dehumanizing process that took forever, we received $170.00 worth, but it felt like a million dollars to us. Regardless of how much money we had in our past, nothing else mattered at that moment. So, we all jumped into the car so fast; I don't even think we closed the doors, went straight to Walmart, and experienced the privilege of buying non-donated groceries.

Although I previously earned what many would consider great money, I was now unemployed. This Lone Star card was an answer to many prayers. We felt blessed and fortunate to be eating, and the eating was good. All praises are to God. For God is good all the time, and all the time, God is good.

ANGRY

"You're an embarrassment to your family and yourself. You're not ready for prime-time; you just think you are. You can't make a consistent living. You're falling further and further behind every day on your bills. You've wasted so much time until now; there's none left anymore. What the hell do you think you're doing? Dying."

For me, I don't want to hear anymore, "Well, it just wasn't meant for you...something better is coming along soon." It all sounds so repetitive; it's just something others say to make you feel better as they attempt to soften your increasingly brutal blows of failure. I don't want to hear, "Well, the Lord was just protecting you from something. You watch.

The next thing will be better than this one," anymore. Hmmm. I cannot deal with the 'why this' or 'why that' again. I have asked the questions, yet I don't get any answers. I have prayed until I have knee burns. All my prayers began to sound the same. In fact, I finally found myself in a place where I could not even pray anymore.

I am alone and becoming even more bitter. I have finally realized that I will not escape this hellhole and miraculously receive that long-awaited phone call making all my dreams come true. I have believed until I cannot believe anymore, yet if I stop believing, I may as well die right here, which is what I feel like doing anyway.

Maybe it's my faith or lack of it, that's making me feel so bad. How can faith make you feel bad? Because for it to work, your spirit has to accept the reality of what it cannot see. You must believe in a favorable outcome, but deep inside, a tiny shred of doubt lies in wait, making you fear what could be the depressing flip side of reality. I have read books, listened to motivational speakers, preaching tapes, church services, and gospel music. I have also made vows, paid tithes, watched videos, prayed more, been prayed for and prayed with, and meditated, yet I remain trapped in a living hell I cannot seem to escape.

I really don't understand, and I don't even know what to think. At this point, I feel lost. I believe that all of this standing still and marking time has only been a slow walk to life's gas chamber, under the guise of the Lord sustaining me; sustaining me for what? If it is the Lord, why doesn't he kill my family and me off right now instead of making us go through all this hell! Day after day, there always seems to be one more disappointment. One more hit. One more promise of something that never materializes. Just one phone call away from employment that never happens. Just one more interview with another promise, a catch, a hitch. I'm done! I truly don't understand. I've been told that God is not sadistic, but is that true? Others say, "Oh, he's just doing it for your good." Is that right?

Sometimes, I genuinely don't know what to think or believe. I really would like just to stop thinking or believing altogether. Maybe God's not doing anything. Perhaps He has me in this stupid holding pattern for nothing. Maybe I'm like a human hamster on His heavenly treadmill, and He's sitting somewhere watching me go through the motions, or maybe He's even left the room, and I'm supposed to run until he gets back, just so the end will all be the same, absolutely nothing.

Or maybe it's all just me. Perhaps I expect life to be fair, and it isn't. Maybe I'm under some heavenly illusion that if I read my Bible, say my prayers, and be good, I'll have this heavenly hotline straight to God when I get into trouble. Believe me; it doesn't happen that way. Am I hurting? Yes. Right now, I'm in bleeding pain. Am I numb? Most definitely. Do I blame anyone? Yes. I blame myself.

Right now, I don't like who I am, what I am, or what I think. Why did my mother have to teach me to love Jesus? Why does it sometimes feel as if I was cursed rather than blessed? Right now, I cannot answer that. All I know is that my life has left a trail of failure debris over the years that I can never repair. I now feel like just another unemployed no-chance-taking-washed-up man who believes he's somebody special. Well, life has kicked my ass and showed me just how 'non-special' I truly am. I am a nobody. I am broke, rejected, and I see little hope at this point.

I don't want to hear from my do-good acquaintances who want to listen to the gory details of my life. They just want the 411 of what's really happening. "Can I pray for you, brother?" No! But can you get me a job? Can you help me sneak up on a paycheck, help me get my life back? Can you help me do that?

I don't want to hear any more from the 'play-it-safers who still have all the comforts of life intact. Those who fail to venture outside the comfort of their status quo lives. Why does it have to be me who does?

Maybe it's because they have been chosen or covered by the blood and not cursed like my ass. I don't know, but whatever the reason for my downward spiral into darkness and despair, I wish I could say, but in all my praying and weeping and moaning and hoping and wishing and waiting, I have yet to uncover any real solutions. God must be out to lunch and not returning calls. I guess he's disconnected that heavenly hotline. I've left Him a stack of messages. Is He avoiding me?

At this point, I feel doomed and defeated. I feel dead inside. I can't cry, nor can I pray anymore. I don't even know if I want to. I feel as though even if there is something good around the corner left up to me, I'll blow the opportunity. So, what's the use? Oh, am I trying to feel sorry for myself? Am I? No, of course not. It's just that there has been nothing good in my life that has come to fruition. No prophet, no preacher, no friend, no one has even passed along a good word that has come true. So, what I now believe is the lie being projected across the big screen T.V. of my life.

Continual disappointment leads to bitterness, and my bitterness has turned to anger. Right now, I am both. I wish I knew what was happening to me. My soul is in turmoil, and I don't want to hear any preaching. I don't want to read the Word of God anymore. I don't want people to try and rescue me from my thoughts or myself. I just want to hate the current environment and the awful state of my life, the stench of failure, the vomit of being broken, the dishonesty of people, and the curse that can come with having a divine gift.

Right now, I do not like my life. I don't like what being associated with me does to others in my life who depend on me. If I am honest with myself enough to admit how good I am at something, I can also admit just my deficiencies too, and right now, I suck, and I don't mind saying it. I don't want to repeat more affirmations or cheesy phrases at this point. Even If I did, I probably wouldn't believe them. At this moment, everything is a lie; people are lies, and I must admit, I am a lie too. I see others as walking billboards of self-promoting propaganda seeking new and unassuming recruits to abuse or take advantage of.

Maybe all of this negative shit-talking will get me nowhere, but one thing's for sure, everything I've done so far sure hasn't gotten me anywhere either. So, what's the difference? What's the use? Hurt is hurt, and right now, I am hurting. There's just no way around it. I'm done. What else can I do? Go on a 12 day fast? Hold an all-night prayer vigil, or make a deal with Darth Vader? **What? What? What?**

"When I am open to prayer, to hearing your voice, to being obedient, but still do know the answer to the questions, then, what?"

What?

Now what oh Lord, now what? Now that I know, now what? You have given me insight and pulled me up from the depths of despair and brokenness, but now, what?

It's not that I don't believe in your word, and please know that this is not my vain attempt at being disobedient. It's not even that I question your will for my life, but right now, I'd just like to know what?

What now? What next? What do I do? What should I be doing? What are you doing with me? What are you doing to me? What is happening? What is going to happen? What do I do to stay afloat, to survive and pay my bills? What Lord? What Lord? Please tell me, what?

I heard your message; I hear your voice. Instead of pulling away from you I drew nearer. Even in the mist of this desert, my brokenness, my Lodebar, my pain, my hurt, my despair...the burning question still remaining in my mind is...what?

Oh God. Is my **crying out** in pain reducing the length of my sentence? Does it make the agony of going through these terrible trials any less, or is it just part of the process? My faith, my faith, oh it is my **faith that keeps me going** even though my heart grows faint?

Oh my God, in agony, I cry. What, when, and most of all, why? **Only you know the answers.** Forever your servant.

What is in your hand?

What is in my hand? Lord, what is in my hand, and what is it that I am to do with it? I cannot and do not understand just what I am to do, where I am to go, or how I will get there. Again, what, dear Lord, what? I am surrounded on all fronts, trying to figure out just what strategy to use. I am out of ideas, options, and choices.

I have already given it over to you. What else am I supposed to do? While all around me, everything is sinking and falling apart, what am I supposed to do? Every day I struggle to stay focused, on task, filled, ready, motivated, renewed, energized, spiritually fed, and enthused. But I have reached a place where I cannot do it anymore! I am broken. My load is too heavy. I cannot go any further, nor do I want to. I am sick, yet I still have a tiny grain of faith left. Is that enough? I still have hope in my eternal Father. I still believe that no one can help me but the Lord.

Lord, why do you allow such calamities to befall me? I have no idea, yet I have every idea. I know I am being polished in the furnace of adversity like pure gold, yet I do not enjoy the process. My mind, soul, and spirit are weak. I am broken further than I ever thought I could be. Each day becomes harder and harder to get out of bed—my body aches. My shoulders are sore. My thoughts are riddled with the leftover frustration and anxiety that only the headache from brokenness brings. I feel like a warrior without a battle, yet I face the most extraordinary battle I have ever fought.

Please, I beg you, do not break me any further, even though in my heart I know it isn't my call. I am a sinner who cannot walk in the expected ways of the Lord, for you know that I am not perfect. It is only your grace and mercy that can see me through. But until my release, I suffer. I suffer in brokenness, yet there is abundant life all around me. I experience wealth while at the same time, I experience failure and lack. I am at the top and bottom of life at the same time while hanging precariously by a thread. I see consistency even though I am inconsistent.

I feel spiritual while at the same time experiencing carnality. I am a success, yet I can see, feel, and smell the rank stench of failure and a reputation in ruin. Now all I want to do is cry. All I want to do is stop standing, stop being strong, stop having to be responsible, stop playing all the roles I have to play, at least for a little while, just for a day or a moment.

On this day, I don't want to be responsible for a family, my bills, or even my life. As selfish as it may sound, I just want a release, just for a moment. But as you know, my family always comes before me. Besides, I cannot imagine life without them. But for once, I would like to let my guard down from the pressures of life, from struggling and having to stand—I want a release, not for long, but just for a little while. I cannot pay my mortgage, the car payments, the credit cards, or even the phone. I cannot provide insurance or food for my family.

It is up to you, Lord. Only you can truly understand. I am without a confidant, advisor, or friend. What, Lord? What is it that you would have me do with this thing in my hand? What? Just let me know! Tell me, what must I do with it? I am surrounded by this tsunami of life. I am drowning from life in peril with no visible means of escape.

My enemies are waiting for the signal to annihilate me, kill me, tear my flesh to pieces, and disgrace me. I feel so close to death, yet I still feel so close to abundant life. In the gut of my body, I am in pain. I can almost feel the daggers piercing my being. I feel the past knives of betrayal, the angry fists that beat upon my face representing the sweet lies of deception.

It is the Lord who delivers me. He is my hope, my salvation, my rock. He leads me, even when I do not feel like being led. He is there with me, even though, at times, I feel alone. I know that He will never forsake me, leave me, abandon me, release me, dump me, forget about me, neglect me, or separate himself from me. Though my enemies may surround me and bring death within inches, I remain alive. I refuse to die. The spear of defeat has not yet thrust itself into my being. Again, I refuse to die. Being responsible for others and myself can sometimes be more than I can bear, but I know through Christ I can do all things, be all things, and accomplish all things. Yes, I can do all things. I can have all things. I am all things through Christ, who strengthens me.

"For the Lord is good, his mercy is everlasting, and his truth endureth to all generations." Psalms 100:5 KJV

And that includes me.

Amen

Letting Go

Today we had a sale; a garage sale, estate sale, moving sale, heartbreak sale, giving up sale, no longer-can-hang sale, giving-up-our-lives sale, a life-as-we-once-knew-it sale, an embarrassment sale. We placed our most personal and beautiful treasures on display and made others desire them. We propped ourselves up just to look happy, but deep down, there were no words that could ever express what we truly felt.

There were bargains everywhere; a piece representing love here, a tattered heartstring there, that special I don't-want-to-give-it-up-but-I-have-to, piece, that unique item that can never be replaced can be yours at a rock-bottom price, including the famous 'Joy Chair;' the chair I used to rock my young son to sleep in. Please underbid, just so I can say, "No, I can't take that." Although I am desperate, I won't let it show. Just take it and go. You'll never know.

"Would you take twenty-five for that?" To yourself, you answer, "No," because the emotional value is worth a thousand. The truth is, you can't hold on to it, so you say,

"I'll take thirty-five. You get thirty and move on."

Today, we displayed pieces of a family's heart scattered on the driveway of an upscale house in an upscale neighborhood, displaying exclusive items from an upscale life we can no longer hold onto. What we collect at the end of the day will further reduce our previous life to fragments. The pain of letting go is beyond emotional.
Just let go.

"Whatever that thing is that you think you love so much, sometimes trying to hold onto it is futile. When the time comes, you have to let go."

Steven LeMons

Moving
Moving
Moving

I sit and wait, looking around at everything that once was. The treasures I struggled to acquire. The things that made my soul feel special both inside and out are now all dismantled; yet I wait.

The spirit of laughter and life that lived in this space is no more. The smiles, the voices, and love that once filled these rooms are now merely an echo.

The pink walls of my daughter's bedroom, the blue in my son's, the stairwell we descended, and the kitchen where meals brought us together will soon make memories for someone else.

We've gone as far as we can go. I now sit here, trying to hide the pain while waiting on the movers.

Part II.
Love

love

Sometimes love hangs only by a thread. But sometimes a thread is all you need.

"There cannot be true love without trust, and there can be no trust without truth."
Steven LeMons

You warm my soul with such intense loving energy; I find myself sensually aroused when thinking of you. You touch my heart in ways I never knew possible. Your love leaves me breathless. I do not have enough words to adequately explain my feelings for you. My passion runs deep. Far more profound than a parting glance or superficial flirtation. Your vocal phrases, soft tonality, stimulating intellect, romantic and inviting smile, witty sense of humor, breathtaking sensuality, and spiritual compatibility provide a haven for my broken soul. You were made for me. You are my soulmate. So many nights in my loneliness, I longed and ached for you. It is complete and real when I think of making love to you. I give myself totally and completely to you. Neither my passion nor body can lie. I move in harmony with you and you with me. Your mind, body, soul, and emotions all become one with mine. I am yours and here to share your deepest thoughts and most intimate desires. I am here to serve you and meet you where you are—to understand you, your emotions, and your longings. I crave you, your touch, your tenderness, your fragrance, and the softness of your lips. You fill the wounds of my heart with a love I have never known. What have you done to me? What have I done to you? I surely do not know. And if I should lose this moment, I will never be the same, for you have truly marked my heart. I will forever love the beauty within you because it has forever changed me.

Living Without

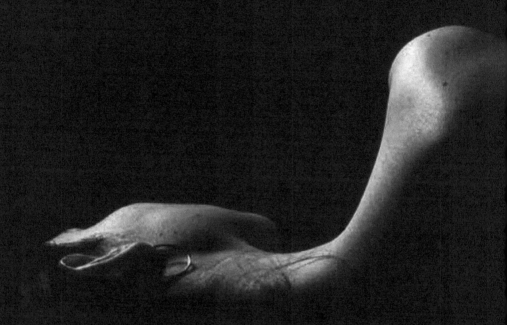

There I was, managing and suppressing my pain with only ragged remnants of what remained of my tattered emotions and unproductively dull life. I was facilitating and nurturing my quasi-self-induced coping program. I was going through the motions, trying with everything inside myself to find the positive side of life, but I couldn't.

I was anesthetizing myself through the dull, tedious drudgery of consistency, boredom, and routine, as opposed to capturing the heightened optimistic inspiration my spirit longed for; the living-out-loudism I knew existed within my soul. I was not giving up but wanting to. Not giving in, yet feeling the overall weight of my mundane existence surrounding and crushing me so, until I felt my inner frame creaking and bowing under the overwhelming stress and strain of a life weighed down by the invisible misery, I became accustomed to. I had learned to cope, compromise, and compartmentalize my life. I trained myself to endure, nothing else.

I neatly packaged and prioritized my insecurities. I kept my head down and continued moving until it all became a habit. Before my self-induced hibernation, my external laugh was loud, boisterous, and highly contagious. My personality and charm were intoxicating. It was the side of myself everyone saw, heard, and thought people knew but didn't. In fact, they heard my laughter and learned to expect humor even before my physical presence. However, inside, it was me who, in spirit, never allowed laughter to happen. I couldn't. I had forgotten how.

My life had evolved into such an oppressive state until there was never anything to laugh about, so time became my prison. It marched into weeks, months, even years. Its expansiveness could not be measured. It seemed endless. The loud, deafening tick-tocks of my mental clock turned into what seemed like endless hours. Hours turned into days, days into weeks, months, and years. My life seemed to be going around in circles with one disappointment after another. I never got off the treadmill of stagnation.

It was the nasty adversity that defined and enslaved me. In fact, it was this adversity that created the bars solidifying what appeared to be my endless prison sentence and relationship abstinence. At night, I found myself chasing the illusion of sleep, yet sleep continued to elude me.

In the small wee hours of the morning, I finally succumbed, exhaustion being the victor. I found it difficult to turn off the sounds, pictures, and tormenting visions swirling around inside my aching mind of how a life without loneliness could be. For me, there was no up, nor down, no win, no lose, no good, no evil, no boundaries, nor existence. There never were any days of sunshine, only the ever-present and forever looming darkness of long oppressive nights. It was the night that magnified the exacerbation and frustration lying just beneath the surface of my sad, lonely, and pathetic existence. When would it ever end, I wondered?

Then, when I least expected it and without cause or expectation, came you. Immediately and with quiet and seductive fanfare, you made your entrance. Your presence was like a thousand-watt light bulb, killing off the darkness and shattering it into a million pieces. You instantaneously illuminated and electrified everything in my life, from the longest hair on my head to the soles of my tired aching feet. Your presence was like the force of a thousand raging rivers, penetrating the deepest, most hidden places in my mind and body and with a current so strong, once experienced, I could never imagine living without it.

Your attraction to me was unexpected; life would never be the same. An intense glance in my direction, the way you made the environment move at your whim, the subtle breeze you created that followed your stride aroused me. I was done. I could not resist your charm, your style, your smile, your humor, your smell, your hands, your hair, your spirit, and the place in my heart you grew to possess. Your presence was invigorating and intoxicating beyond words. Every part of my mind, body, and soul was drunk for you. I desired you. I found myself addicted to you. For me, there was no turning back. My now awakened spirit became hypersensitive. You were my soulmate.

What did you see in me that attracted you? What did I do to bring these feelings out in you? You made me display my true colors. Like inhaling second-hand smoke from an illegal substance, I became high from your very presence. My thoughts began to embrace the slight possibility of what it would be like, feel like, and look like if you became part of my life. You made me feel things that I had never felt before. You made me breathe and want to live again. The scabs that once covered my eyes had dissolved, and the permanent blinders I wore for so long were finally peeled off. I could see again.

The blissful and rejuvenating winds of love catapulted me into an uncontrollable orbit. Gravity could no longer hold me. I soared higher than I had ever imagined. Your spirit elevated me up through the clouds and into the heavens. I felt a sense of weightlessness. I began to view life as I'd never seen it before. As our relationship deepened, every day, I wanted more of you. I was hooked. The warm rays from your soft kisses and gentle touches from your finely-manicured hands penetrated the thick walls of loneliness that, up until now, I never realized how much I had taken ownership. These walls formed a thick crust of armor I used to protect myself. Their strength filtered out any possibility of me ever connecting with the real side of me.

You allowed me to uncover a beautiful side of mine I once knew. Now, I could see the same in another, in you. That's what you did. Like being laser-focused on a target, you shined your brilliant light into the darkest corners of my blackened and distorted soul. Like the rays of the sun melting fresh snow from a rooftop, I submitted and committed myself to the invitation of your dance. Like Mary Shelly's character Frankenstein, I found myself being brought back to life. I now realize that I am human and still possess the God-given capacity to feel and be loved.

We shared the simplicity of laughter, sometimes so hard until all my negativity had to bow. There was no place for the pain to reside or exist; it had to leave. It was you who helped me pull back the tattered covers created by numbness and nothingness to see what the power of love really could do. Your sweet verbal balm and refreshing words encouraged my soul yet discouraged my weaknesses. Is this what freedom, liberation, joy, and love feel like? Damn! I could do this forever.

You awakened my life in ways I had long since believed were never possible; until now. Until now, I didn't realize flowers had colors, trees actually bloom, and birds still sing. I never thought to appreciate the beauty of a sunset until I saw one with you. I had buried the realization of how powerful, sensational, and erotic touch from a woman could be until now. You breathed upon my neck and awakened an avalanche of chills that felt like the energy of 100,000 self-made electrical volts going down my spine.

Every pore on my body opened wide and connected with you. I tingled uncontrollably! I had become whole again. For once in my life, my mind, body, spirit, and soul came together simultaneously, colliding as if they were the raw ingredients used to create the entire universe. Like the force of a never-ending orgasm nurtured from the result of prolonged abstinence, only to connect at the appointed time with the body of a soulmate, I cried out in suppressed ecstasy. With the deepest of emotion, I quivered. I was left in awe and breathlessness.

Then it happened. In the blink of an eye, it all came to an end. My dream, which had embraced an unbelievable reality, died as quickly as it had manifested. What did I do? I can fix it; this can't be over; it just can't be. Why didn't you tell me you came with strings attached? How could you ever do this to me? How could I ever allow you or anyone else to do this to me? How could anyone ever awaken the dormant unhappy, unnoticeable, insecure, broken me in the first place?

I now find myself shattered into a million pieces. I am now experiencing what light feels like when it is diminished. I now find myself mystified in the surrounding darkness. I am uncontrollably falling from my imaginary mountain—and at breakneck speed. It seems as if the beauty of the sun was beaten into submission by the blackness of the night.

My sunny days have now disappeared, gone forever. A reckless army of demons has been dispatched from hell to destroy me. I am devasted and do not know how to be. Was it better for me to have remained as I was than relearn how to feel, breathe, see, and love again? I waited to exhale and finally did, only to find death waiting to slay me. Like a parched plant gasping and starving from the lack of rejuvenation and restoration only water and light brings, I was dying too, yet I managed and coped.

Before you, despite myself, I survived. You came to me in the perfect package. You were my hemlock, complete with the sweet taste of golden honey, my Kool-Aid of death, my own private hellion, my soul seducer and tormentor. You cloaked yourself in extraordinary charm, seductive words, and stunning beauty, when all the while knowing, I was just another temporary conquest.

Once you possessed the beauty of my soul, for you, it was time to move on to the next unassuming victim. Oh, how do I now ache from the lack of this addictive drug in the form of a woman! Why do I crave the inexplicable imitation of joy I became so accustomed to? Like an insatiable form of crack cocaine, I bought your sweet song, your words, your eyes, and your smile. I was seduced by you and the beauty of your lies. I snorted your charm, injected your intimacy, and smoked your seduction. I now am hopelessly addicted and suffering the consequences.

My withdrawals are menacing, and my mental and physical release of you reluctant. I tremble, not wanting to let go. I resist, as I still hold firmly with everything in me. I am torn. I refuse to let go even though you have already released me. I see only where you once were. Your fragrance still lingers on the pillow where you slept; the glass you drank from, the chair you sat, your brush with strands of hair; all pieces of a heart you left behind. Here it comes; I'm again beginning to see and feel the emptiness that at one time consumed me. I have failed. You have taken what I saw as your love-beyond-measure, your heart, your joy, your ambiance, and energy, all gone.

The darkness is now even darker. The hole from whence I came is now deeper. The winds that once howled in the night are now much colder than ever, and so am I. What once took me to a climactic and heated passion is no more. I again settle back into my self-induced state of rigor. My spirit now lives in anger, blaming the physical me for allowing itself to have ever been compromised and re-broken. "You should have protected us better," my spirit cries.

There is nothing more painful than a broken spirit. My heart, listening, is compelled to agree. However, my mind has still yet to be convinced; so, it commits the only act or crime it knows, waiting in agony, yet rationalizing with itself and living in denial of this catastrophic event. Foolishly, it believes she will return. My parts are scattered. My mind, soul, spirit, and body are all at war with themselves. I make useless but deliberate attempts at piecing each collected piece of myself back together while all the time realizing none of them will ever fit the way they once had. I refuse to accept the pain of this reality. Like an atomic bomb that annihilates an entire city, when it's a heart, there is also nothing left but collateral damage. Every part of me has been obliterated.

Was it better to have never loved than to bask in the captivation of it and now be forced to live without it? Was it better to have experienced the euphoric heights of amorous play or never embrace the innocent, childlike insanity of folly at all? I continue to agonize, yet I will forever miss you. Although my heart is shattered into a million pieces, I will not claim defeat because I still love you. I miss you so much.

Please come back.

sometimes

sometimes
it seems
as if
neither one of us
will ever
breathe again.
but we will.
i have faith in God
and I have faith

Checkmate

I am now, and have always
been on your side more than
you will ever know.

Every move of my heart that I
Make doesn't involve strategy
or a motive.

The fight between us has to
stop. Let's just live and let
live; know that in love, the only
checkmate is sacrifice…
not gotcha.

Special

You are truly something else. God really knew what he was doing when he selected the clay to create you. Clad in your purposeful, divine, wisdomatic, and intellectual beauty, you have evolved into a graceful and elegant example of Godly artistry, the divine substance, and a physical presence that could make a goddess insecure. Wow! Is this the woman I have come to admire?

Am I being a little too presumptuous in how I interpret, visualize, or feel you? Have I become blinded by the newness and power of your uniqueness in such a short amount of time, or have you with mine? Could it be that my soul is just starving for something so raw and essential to my essence and existence that I project a burning need? Or am I guilty of reflecting a desire of something so real that I reflect it upon you, just hoping you could be my true soulmate, the one who only comes along once in a lifetime?

No, I am certainly not suffering from a runaway imagination, but what I do know is when my heart sees the reflection of its opposite self-revealed through another, my spirit stirs from the vibrations and intoxicating energy. Even though opposites do attract, likeness also recognizes and attracts likeness. It acknowledges the nature of itself when it exists in another individual.

My spirit secretly whispers insights that answer questions I would like to ask you but haven't. Why? Because in my heart, I already know the answers. To truly embrace such a thing, how then should I be? What should I think? Are you live, or are you a virtual facsimile created by my mind? Are we just two people passing through time on a temporary path-crossing journey to a destination holding our true realities? Or, have we found ourselves temporarily at a time-traveler's weigh station where we both have stopped long enough to put down our life bags and take a breather from this tiring universal journey? Or, could this be the beginning of where one journey ends and another truly begins for you and I?

You are more woman than I have ever had, yet could you be the woman I would love to spend the rest of my life with? Could you be the soulmate of my dreams? The one who at her core is not just about the act, but also the art of making love, vulnerability, respect, and being accepted for who she is by someone who truly knows, loves, and appreciates her essence? Could this be you? If so, I may not know where you are going, but I sure look forward to going there with you.

Stay blessed.

blinded

for years
I was blinded by all the love
I had for you and what I believed
was there, but when I
finally took off the mask of denial and
tinted glasses that hid the reality
of who was really there,
I did not like who I saw.

When I came home today,
home was gone.
No kids, no wife, no love, no life, only deafening
silence. Get used to it, buddy; it is what it is.
That may be right, but hell, I won't go without a
fight.
Florescent lights humming in the silence
make deafening noises when you're alone,
with nothing but your thoughts.
Where did we go wrong?
It's all your fault, not mine, but yours.
I should never have said it; I wish you would; we go
back and forth in the argument.
Anger overpowers and emasculates the soul. It's
beyond cold.
I'm sorry you can't see that I'm bleeding pain, yet
I'm sure you're doing the same; what a damn
shame, we both are to blame
this is insane.
The end of a life we once knew is now here, only a
barren landscape of guilt and shame. Nothing
remains.
The love in your spirit for me has died, and I can no
longer hang on to you. What do we do?
It's done.
Home is gone.

No matter where I go or whatever I do,
I will always pray for you.
I will pray for both your healing and mine.
I will pray for your protection, your
strength, and that you ultimately receive the
best God has for you and that you live your
best life.

Regardless of Whatever we believe about
each other or wherever we ultimately end up
in the world, prayer crosses all boundaries.
I will always pray for you.

When the solitude of sleep just doesn't come. During these hours, my mind finds itself drifting in deep thought, recalling places, events, and people I find important. At this hour, it is you I am thinking of. How interesting. First, I find myself constantly staring at the beauty of your pictures as though they were enough. In vain attempts at calming myself by the sweetness of music, one thing leads to another, then comes imagination, and ultimately, this writing. Silly, right? Anyway, I realize you may not care for my kind of music, for that remains to be seen; however, to me, this song I send to you ties a bow around the feelings I have for you. Please, don't misunderstand; I wouldn't make any attempt at manipulating your thoughts; however, being truthful, my feelings come from an old dusty box and will never be the same again. That's the deal. Silly, right?

wisdom

Part
III
Wisdom

*"For those humbled, enlightened, and often
reluctant instruments who have
endured the pain of being broken,
wisdom reflects the fruits of your labour."*
Steven LeMons

weight

With the addition of weight, you are
positioned to be stretched.

And the more stretched you become
the more you grow.

Through stretching and growth there is
considerable pain.

Continuous growth requires working
through the pain, not running away
from it.

The heavier the weight, the stronger you
become. The stronger you become,
the more weight you can endure.

By continuing to endure the weight, the pain,
and not fainting, you will not see the same
person but a better one when looking back at
yourself over time.

wait

During a particular summer, and with what seemed like a very long unemployment spell, a friend was nice enough to offer me a pair of free tickets to the Six Flags Over Texas amusement park. What a welcomed relief it was. If you're like me, what could be more exciting than getting free tickets to an amusement park, especially Six Flags? So, what if we didn't have money and had to smuggle our own water and snacks inside the park? What the heck? We were at Six Flags, and that's all that mattered. We would ride the attractions until our heart's content. The lucky companion of the day accompanying me on this adventure was my son, Jacob.

Both of us were committed to spending some much-needed father-son time together on this day. It would be just the two of us, taking a break from the insanity of life to have fun. We could act as silly as we both wanted and push our fear of riding scary rides to their limits. I was always fascinated by going to carnivals and amusement parks as a kid. I still vividly remember when the traveling amusements would come to our neighborhood. I was looking forward to riding attractions that would blow my hair straight back on my head, and for me, that would be pretty hard to do.

The carnies would set up what seemed like an entire circus in an empty parking lot or open field. You would see big tractor-trailer trucks, RVs, and an assortment of other vehicles, all parked throughout the makeshift city. I could hear the sound of generators humming, see bright neon lights, and jump over the thick black taped-down electrical cables that snaked their way throughout the walking areas. Try as they might covering them up, we all knew they were the lifelines that connected all the machines necessary for having a great time.

Let's not forget the music from the carousel; it has always been an amusement park staple. For whatever reason, the carousel music played in amusement parks today still evokes the same memories and sounds I remember as a child. Watching the carousel horses go round and round was the cherry on top of the experience that made amusement parks special. And when it came to food, even if I had just eaten dinner, I always found myself hungry again for a giant corny dog or hotdog, slathered in mustard, catsup, and topped with onions.

The smell of cotton candy, funnel cakes, and popcorn was appetizingly intoxicating. Oh, let's get sucked in by a carnival vendor, "I just know we could win one of those giant bears." Their monotonous yet infectious voices generate excitement from bystanders during their attempts at hustling you into an odds game you could not possibly win. But for that large brown teddy bear tilted in the back, you would definitely try. I always wanted to ride the colorful helicopters that went around in circles like a carousel, occasionally rising and falling, as they gave you the false sensation and thrill of a flight. Even though we did not ride many of the attractions, it still was fun just being there.

And what's an amusement park without a rickety roller coaster? You know, the barely held together ones looking as if they would come apart at any minute. Who cared if it was safe or not? I don't even think the thought of safety crossed our minds, but it sure brought out the screams and smiles from every kid or adult brave enough to ride it. Even though my mother couldn't afford to pay for many rides, the ones my brothers and I experienced gave us an adrenaline rush that, to this day, we still remember. The truth is, I was an adrenaline junkie when it came to fast rides.

But that was then, and this is now. Finally, I looked forward to doing it all again, but this time with Jacob. Although this all sounded great in theory, there was only one problem with this grandiose vision I had. Not only was Jacob not interested in the same things, or even the types of rides I was, he wasn't exactly thrilled about amusement parks in general either. He didn't like the crowds, heat, noise, rides, or other things associated with such places. You see, Jacob is the type of kid who would instead study physics and the what-makes-it-go-G-force principles of a roller coaster than ride it.

So, after entering the park and having fruitless attempts at trying to convince him to ride several rides he had no interest in, Jacob proceeded to hit me with a bombshell I didn't see coming. "Dad, I don't want you to be disappointed at me for not wanting to ride anything. But I don't like these kinds of rides." Huh! Wait just a minute. Hold the bus! In so many words, the boy just told me that he could care less about the unspoken nostalgic ride-a-rocket crap I found so sentimental. So, what's a dad to do?

I feel for the guy who spends his entire life playing sports or at least being a sideline quarterback throughout his high school, college, or pro career, only to have a son who could care less about football. It's Sunday, and Dad can't wait to sit down in front of the big screen to watch the 49ers versus the Cowboys with his 10-year-old son. With popcorn, Cheetos, and drink in hand, Dad discovers his son has no interest whatsoever in the game but would rather be in his room listening to Mozart while conducting his imaginary orchestra.

For some, this attitude would be considered a cardinal sin and surpasses all levels of macho disappointment. For many, it could even have lifetime consequences. But not for my son. It didn't matter to me because I loved him for who he is, as I do each of my children. As for Jacob, it was all okay; however, upon seeing the look in his eyes, I had little choice but to accept his words. There was no forcing, belittling, or making him feel worse than he already did. I understood. I mean, I really did understand.

So, I assured him that I wasn't angry, nor could I be disappointed in him for being honest. However, armed with the new information he provided, we both had to start from square one—time for plan B. So, we proceeded to walk over and look at the park map in hopes of getting a new idea. That's when a particular ride on the map caught Jacob's eye. "Dad, what's the 'Mini Mine Train?" Surprised by his question, I answered, Well, Jake, it's a small roller coaster. "Can kids ride it?" Sure, I replied. "Can we ride it?" If you'd like Jake, but it's all the way on the other side of the park. It's quite a walk from here. If we walk over there, are you sure you'll ride it? "Yes, Dad, I'll ride it." Yes! I thought to myself. Now, I did tell him that the Mini Mine train was a roller coaster, but as I recall having ridden this ride once before, I remember it was awfully fast. But I surmised that once he saw it, he could make up his own mind if he wanted to ride it or not.

So off we went, passing each of my dangerously favorite rides. But after all, this wasn't about me. It was about being with my son, and that's what mattered most. Just the fact that he decided what he wanted to do was enough to satisfy me. When we finally arrived at the other side of the park, an arrow directed us to the Mini Mine Train. I thought to myself, *"Steven, this could be a fun ride for Jake."* Now, even though we'd walked all the way to the other side of the park and were now going through the ride's turnstile, I could still sense Jacob's slight discomfort. As he stood in line dressed in blue shorts, an orange and blue striped short-sleeved shirt, and his signature blue Fubu baseball cap, he was the epitome of a Black poster child for some family T.V. show or kid's product.

At that time, I really wanted to know what was going through Jacob's mind. Maybe he felt that he'd come too far to back out now, or perhaps, in his mind, disappointment wasn't a second option, or perhaps all was fine, and he was displaying his take-the-bull-by-the-horns, Nike, just-do-it look on his face. Whichever it was, I will never know. However, he did find comfort in knowing that there were many kids in the line, some younger than himself.

The waiting line was relatively short, so it wasn't long before we were standing in the short end of the queue line, waiting for the cars to stop so we could jump in. By now, I noticed a spark in Jacob's eyes, almost a sign that he was anticipating his bold new walk on the wild side. As the cars came to a complete stop and riders exited, from the looks on their faces, they were not disappointed. It seemed they all enjoyed the ride. Great! I just knew that once my son experienced the fun from riding in these little metal cars, he'd be hooked. Not only would he do it once, but he'd also want to do it again and again.

We finally sat down and took our places inside the ride. We were lucky; our car was the last one. Great position, right? As the ride attendant pulled down the safety bar and made sure everyone was safely inside, I realized it wasn't as easy to fit all of me inside the small ride as it used to be. But somehow, I managed. Now that everyone was finally locked in, the cars slowly began to roll. The air was fresh and breezy, and it felt good on my face.

Jacob was looking at me with a slightly nervous but apprehensive smile, almost as if he didn't know whether he should like the sensation or not. He acted as if he was beginning to loosen up a bit, just waiting for the 'fun ball' to drop. I was okay with that. As we rounded the first corner, the coaster took a slight dip that gently made our stomachs float. I thought to myself; this is going to be great. From the looks on my son's face, he thought so too. As with any roller coaster, there had to be an incline to gain speed, and with this ride, that was no exception.

As the cars latched onto the incline's chain and gradually went higher and higher, I could feel the coaster being pulled and jerked. The incline was gradual and steep. I could tell its effect would make this a great experience. The higher our climb, the better our view of the surrounding area. We could now see a vast portion of the park. Once the coaster finally crested the top of the hill, all control was lost once gravity took over. The Mini Mine Train was fast and furious. It was a 100% adrenaline rush!

At breakneck speed, we hurtled down the tracks toward the bottom of the hill. The screams and laughter of the riders were loud and infectious. We could hear them in the back where we sat. I even found myself being tossed around and letting out an occasional 'whoa' as my body felt the effects of weightlessness. We could see the cars in front of us as they turned and jerked their way around the tracks, knowing that within the next second, we would experience the same sensations. The experience took me back to a simpler and more carefree time in life. But as with every roller coaster, there are high and low hills.

This one was no exception. As we zoomed from the top of the hill toward its bottom, the coaster took a hard bank to the left and then to the right, and that's when it happened—my son's blue Fubu hat flew off. At about 50 miles per hour, the wind just ripped it right off his head. *Pow*, in a second, it was gone. And within those few seconds, life changed. The hat took a flight somewhere within the large amusement park real estate expanse known as Six Flags Over Texas.

The fact is that people lose things every day; hats, caps, sunglasses, and all possessions at parks, malls, theaters, airports, and especially at amusement parks. However, knowing my son, the first about him is that Jacob is no ordinary kid, and second, this was no ordinary hat. This cap was special. His mother bought it for him very early in his childhood. He identified with it on some strange yet affectionate level. It was something like his good luck charm. This hat was just as important to him as an arm, leg, even his nose. It seemed to have been stitched into his DNA. In other words, it was his prized possession, and he unconditionally loved it.

At the exact moment of the unavoidable incident, I heard a cry from my son I had never heard before. Although I had heard him cry previously, it was never like the sound he had just made. This one sounded almost as if someone had stuck a dagger in his body, and he was crying out in excruciating pain. It sounded practically primal and prehistoric. I had never heard this sound before, nor did I ever desire to hear it again.

It was at this point that the tears started streaming across his face. Not vertically like I was used to seeing, but from the sheer speed of the roller coaster, the tears were streaming horizontally. All the while, Jacob was looking at me in hopes that I could fix it, help make it all better, or just make the pain go away, but I couldn't. At that moment, for Jacob and I, everything in our world suddenly stopped—and within an instant, life was in suspended animation. Like some frozen scene from the Matrix movie where time and characters temporarily hover in mid-air. At that point, the ride, the wind, the fun, nothing mattered or even existed.

Since we were only halfway through our ride, what remained was merely a frustrating and painful exercise in torture. "My hat, my hat! Daddy, my hat!" He screamed in terror. For me, there was never a time in my life when as a father, I felt so helpless and unproductive as I did when I tried to comfort my son. Despite my best efforts, there was nothing I could do. Nothing! After what seemed like an eternity and the longest ride in Six Flag history, the coaster finally pulled into its starting point, slowed, and stopped. As the safety bar went up, I couldn't help but see the impact of loss on my son's face.

With every ounce of emotion in his body, he tearfully asked, "Daddy, can we, please, go back and get my hat, please?" No, Jacob, we can't. But let's talk to the ride attendant. Maybe he can help us. We walked over to the young man attending the ride and explained our situation. The attendant informed us that nothing could be done about the hat until the ride closed down for the evening. He also told us maintenance people checked around the rides each night after shutdown for lost items. If they find articles, they turn them into the Lost & Found Department. However, no one was allowed to go and look for it at that moment.

The young man suggested we report the incident to security at the front of the park near the entrance. That was it. From that point on, nothing was the same. The remainder of our visit was a disaster. To make matters worse, I took the last dollars I had for Jacob to play some of the carnival games, hoping he would feel better. By doing so, I think I made it worst.

Jacob attempted to play a game requiring water to be squirted onto a target in hopes of winning a stuffed toy, one he had already picked out. Regardless of how hard he tried (myself included), there was always someone who seemed to come from behind at the last minute to win. Even smaller kids sitting on their parents' laps would come from nowhere at the last second to win a prize. At this point, Jacob looked up at me with disbelief and devastation on his face. As a father, I felt helpless.

"Why is it that I can never win anything, Dad? It just seems like no matter what I do, and no matter how hard I try, I just can't seem to win at anything." Not winning a prize reminded him of the loss of his hat. Again, the tears began to roll down his face. I held his hand and guided him to a bench, where we sat down and talked. I have always viewed these as defining and teachable opportunities.

I believe the next thing that comes from a parent's mouth can sometimes empower or even devastate a child. "Look at me, Jacob," I said, "It's okay; just because you don't win a prize today doesn't mean that you're not a winner. Not at all. Maybe it's just not meant for you to win on this day, but that doesn't mean you won't win tomorrow or even the next day. But what happens when you do win is that the winning is usually bigger, better, and sweeter than anything you could have ever won before. You'll see. The reward you'll get will be better than all the other stuff you've missed today combined."

Looking up at me as though he was trying hard to comprehend my words, Jacob acknowledged me with another question. "Daddy, will I get my hat back?" My answer to him was, "I don't know, Jacob." At this moment, as a parent I attempted to draw from some experience, whether factual or temporarily fabricated, helps soften the blow or prove my point. So, I shared a story. "Jacob, I remember losing a cap myself on a ride." "Did you get it back?" "No, I did not," I said, trying to prepare him with a softer blow, just in case he didn't get his hat back. "Dad, I'm tired. Can we go get something to eat and go home?" "Sure, Jacob," I said. As we made our way to the park's front entrance, another attendant directed us to the Lost & Found office.

As we entered the crowded office, surprisingly, many others were plagued by the unfortunate experience of losing something important to them. One teenage boy whose friend was trying to comfort him was distraught by losing his wallet. A young lady had lost her cell phone, and another had lost her purse. A young man was upset over the loss of his car keys. He had no idea where he lost them. What's worse was the key to his apartment was on the same ring, and he did not have a spare.

Each person experienced hurt, sadness, and frustration from their loss. For some, what should have been a fun day, was now replaced by devastation due to unfortunate events. Finally, it was our turn to state our case. I took the lead by prefacing the incident, "We'd like to report the loss of a hat," I said to the female officer behind the counter. She responded by asking, "Where did you lose it?" Until this incident, I could not understand how anyone could ask this question. If you lost something, it's lost, and you don't know where it is. So, how would you know where you lost it if you consider it lost? It was then that the light came on. Sometimes, people know where and when they lose things, and there are instances when they do not.

However, the question made sense this time because we knew exactly where our item was lost. "We lost it rounding the first major turn off the Mini Mine Train ride," I said. The security officer, who I'm sure after countless hours of hearing stories of loss, was tired but surprisingly still expressed a great deal of empathy and concern about our loss. She wrote down the information and continued asking questions about the description of the cap, its style, color, markings, and so forth.
Jacob stepped up and began answering every question as if he had initiated the entire investigation himself. She restated what the ride attendant had earlier told us; nothing could be done until after the after-hours crew

had swept the area. If Jacob's hat were found, they would return to the Lost & Found office. She would call us, or we could follow up by contacting her. Upon completing the report, she provided us with the contact information to follow up the next day.

That was it. Our day at Six Flags had officially ended. We thanked the officer and walked out of the small office and toward the parking lot. There's a certain irony when you experience devastation in the midst of happiness. It takes a toll on your emotions in ways you cannot quite process. To an eight-year-old, Six Flags is supposed to be one of the happiest places on earth until you experience devastation or disappointment. We walked to the car went home.

The next day began as usual. Jacob did not seem too concerned about his hat; after all, maybe it was still too early, or he was preoccupied playing with a toy and watching television. Whatever the reason, he simply went about his daily routine as if nothing had happened. Unlike adults, children usually have a window of time when they don't think about issues; they seem to put them out of mind. It's not that they forget about them, but for a while, they just leave it alone. It was about 10:30 in the morning when I decided to call the security officer to follow up on the situation.

Dialing the number, I did not know what to expect, but to my surprise, the person answering the phone was the same officer who took our report the following evening. As I refreshed her memory of Jacob and the hat, she responded, "Oh, I remember you two. I was working last night and took your report. You know, when they do sweeps around the rides at night, we usually find anywhere from twelve to fifteen hats. This time, they only found seven, and one of them was your son's." "Really!" I said, being shocked and surprised. "Yes. It was right in the turn, exactly where you said it was. Your description was great. It also helped that Jacob's name was already written inside the hat. Would you like to come and pick it up, or would you prefer we mail it to you free of charge?" I was stunned by her words.

Not only did they find his hat, but they would mail it for free. My reply was, "If it's not too much trouble, would you mind dropping it in the mail. I thought it would be great for Jacob to get something important in the mail with his name on it." "Not at all. I'd be happy to." She proceeded to get our mailing information. I thanked her again and hung up. During this time, Jacob had been in the other room, playing and watching one of his favorite television shows. I called him into the room to give him the great news. He beamed like sunshine. I could tell how delighted he was. It also made me feel great inside to see the expression on his face. However, like most kids, it lasted only for a few minutes, and it was on to something else.

After a moment of basking, he turned around and promptly went back to watching another episode of *Spongebob Squarepants*. A few days later, the package addressed to Jacob arrived from Six Flags. Not only was his hat in the package, but it also included a lovely letter that made us both feel great. The hat had gone full circle. The end of Jacob's life without his prized cap was not to be. All was now well again. He was happy, and so was I, but what I learned from the experience was the lesson of a lifetime. One I still hold deeply in my wisdom pool today, as I explain in the following writing. So, what are you doing while you're waiting on your hat?

Jacob's hat

Lessons I Learned While Waiting on My Hat

It's amazing how our experiences in life have a way of educating and bringing each of us into alignment with principles we should already know and live by but do not. It is only through these humbling experiences that wisdom is acquired. Wisdom is a virtue or trait necessary for a higher quality of life. Borrowing or purchasing it from anyone else is impossible. The lessons learned in pursuing it are as unique as those facing the challenge. Wisdom is earned only through time, experience, and a willingness to grow.

Waiting On Your Hat was written from a personal experience I encountered with my son. This experience presented me with one of life's most valuable, involuntarily lessons I could learn. I find it interesting how life can use any situation, whether through success or adversity, to orchestrate experiences that ultimately inspire us to grow, thrive, and acquire what we need for achieving a higher quality of life. However, during these periods of growth, one must increase in understanding that this is a process.

Although many of us wish to acquire the virtues and positive traits the adversity or process provides, the survival of the process itself is very uncomfortable.

Personal insight can align with opportunities to provide growth from various sources, whether through a song, a movie, or even during a child's play. In my experience, some of the simplest events have set into motion many of my most profound lessons. Jacob's hat, as well as the story, provided just what I needed to learn at that time. What it symbolized to me was a loss. Loss can shatter the fragile balance of our lives, sense of security, and belonging. Its devastation can run deep and derail every aspect of life as we know it. In a child's world, their prized possession may be their bicycle, toy robot, puppy, or even a hat, but to an adult, it's an entirely different story.

When a child suffers the pain of losing one of their prized possessions, it usually signals the end of their world. Their connection with this object is phenomenal. Why? Because the item represents the entire investment of their emotion. There is love attached to the object based on its significance in their life. The raggedy teddy bear with only one eye, the stitching bursting on its arm, and balls of cotton filling oozing from its back represent the child's entire world. Try and replace it if you dare; it doesn't work.

Many of us also find ourselves guilty of similar behaviors in the adult world. Our world is built around things, too. For us, our prized possessions could be our house, job status, finances, credit score, or even our family. For me, my prized possessions became all of those things. Along the way, instead of viewing my accomplishments as gifts, I instead allowed them and my success to define me. I crafted my entire image and value around the things I had acquired. Even though there were errors in my thinking, I believed the more I attained, the easier it was to get what I wanted. I figured that if I could do it, certainly anyone could. I was wrong.

A key lesson I learned about egotistical behavior in a highly competitive sales environment was if I were to compete at higher performance levels and be successful, I had to see myself and the world around me through a different lens. Everyone around me viewed life through the same lens. I had to operate by the same set of rules in my profession. In my mind, it wasn't that I was egotistical; it was normal, my profession demanded it.

Closing sales and production was everything, and everyone around me viewed life through the same lens. In sales, having a take-no-prisoners attitude is essential for survival and success. It's like having the attitude of fighter pilots. If pilots do not believe in themselves or their abilities, they will not survive. They are trained to go into what seems like impossible situations and believe their outcome will be victorious. The same fearless attitude is true for successful people working in commission sales and other pressure-driven professions where talent and communication skills are essential for survival. There is no guaranteed weekly or bi-weekly paycheck in their world to rely on unless you create one for yourself.

I wore this attitude like a finely tailored suit, with fabric consisting of my positive self-talk, outstanding accomplishments, and a take-no-prisoners mindset. This combination knitted together created the perfect material for others to see my success. I wore my suit well, and even though I still held onto small amounts of humility, I made no apologies for my achievement. Are you allowing your 'things' to represent your place in society and on the food chain? Do you find them becoming a reflection of who you are and how you define yourself on the adult scorecard of life? Have they, at the expense of others, become your definition of success by any means necessary? Before you answer these questions, let's delve deeper.

The problem with arrogance, self-centeredness, narcissism, egotism, or any manner of it's-all-about-me'isms, can become so subtle and disguised until once revealed, you may not realize how they have taken up residence in your life. Many of us learn not to live with them; instead, we become them. Over time, they exploit us and take up residence within our personality.

They become what we knowingly and unknowingly reflect, and our possessions in tandem can become the root of what drives our behavior. "I do this all for my family," "I want them to have what I didn't have when I was growing up," "My wife shouldn't have to work, so I provide a higher standard of living," are statements you may have heard yourself, or others else say before. These statements convince us that it's about someone else instead of ourselves. Only after losing what seems most important to us, our status, image, and possessions, do we realize how vanity and ego have taken up residence or even taken over our lives.

I took great pride in providing a top-of-the-food-chain lifestyle for my family. It truly fed my ego to have a high income, five-figure checking account, the best of automobiles, world-class vacations, and practically the best of everything we desired. However, just as Jacob was devastated when he lost his hat, we often become overwhelmed when faced with the loss of our valuables as adults.

Why? Because not only is it how we provide for our family, but for many, especially males, our job becomes an extension of how we sometimes approach the world and conquer it. After losing our 'dream job', we often find life unbearable. In my case, I felt guilty about all these. My job title was another way I saw myself and who I thought I was. Whether director, manager, national consultant, coordinator, specialist, or executive director, my title was unknowingly interwoven into the fabric of my ego suit and identity.

Remember the superhero I mentioned earlier in the book? I became the corporate version of that character in the workplace, cape included. It became my job title, "the director of...." That's who I was and how I identified myself. My identity was tied to my American Express expense account, first-class work travel, the Platinum status airline cards, the concierge level top-of-the-line hotels, and let's not forget the luxury cars and all the other perks that went with this status.

So, how should we react when we lose our home, cars, or financial stability, in simpler words, our stuff? Many of us respond the only way we know. For lack of a better term, we immediately freak out. We want everything to stop and what we've lost immediately restored. If not, we get angry, want to blame someone, and sometimes become overtaken by violent acts.

"There must be some mistake; this can't be happening to me," we reason. Though violence should never be an option, to a point, anger and disappointment may be. However, the true struggle one faces when you hit rock bottom (and at some point, you usually do) is how you handle the situation. How will each of us cope when no one is looking, when we are alone during those periods of embarrassment and frustration? It was during these times that I felt the most helpless. I could not find solutions to my problems, and it wasn't easy to find anyone I could talk to or trust.

It is during these times that you find yourself most vulnerable. At this point, your mind becomes relentlessly filled with questions with no answers on the horizon. During these times, you will discover some of your most valuable lessons. Getting out of your own way then becomes your greatest challenge. The answers to your questions are already there, but anger, resentment, disappointment, and even revenge, can keep these answers, or truth, from being revealed. Although your most important ideas and lessons will come, they reveal themselves once you let go of the negative emotions and open the door of humility to receive them.

If you have an open and honest relationship with God, He may be trying to get your attention because unbeknownst to you, you have been chosen to be reborn and reshaped to become your greater version; the one designed for Him. It is in the involuntary and uncomfortable fiery pit of hell, where wisdom is earned. I call it 'the process'. Right-thinking, sound judgment, and knowledge begin to replace the superficial. This time, you are specifically chosen to fit into a new suit. Through new information and understanding, you will come to know there is a bigger and greater plan at work, one that replaces unnecessary parts of your ego with humility.

Our experiences solidify the true meaning of struggle and our place in it. Wisdom becomes the golden by-product mined from the brokenness of your devastation. It is the earning of wisdom and knowledge that matter most. My first dark night stretched over nine years. During that time, I lost everything I thought was important in my life, including the love and respect of my wife, something during my marriage I could never recover.

Sometimes life just happens, and there is no single individual to blame. Each person you target as an antagonist is only someone chosen to play a starring role in your experience to move you to a place where you could ultimately come face-to-face with yourself. In *Waiting On Your Hat*, there was a point in the story where I was unsuccessful regardless of how hard I tried to comfort Jacob. My words or caresses were not enough to massage away his pain. It was something only he alone had to endure. Adversity custom designs each challenge to fit the recipient, even a child. What one person may find challenging, another may see as, "I sure wish I had your problems," however, problem distribution usually doesn't work that way. Therefore, ultimately, no one gets away with anything that doesn't, at one time, take them to the very edge of their life.

It's as if you're a passenger in a car being driven out of control. As it moves recklessly closer toward the edge of a cliff, it is only then when you realize how extremely fragile your life is. In that moment you come to realize how not in control you are. But, like 99.9% pure gold refined in a fiery furnace, wisdom is forged and earned through these harrowing and adverse experiences that take us to life's scary edge.

Crafted from the depths of your despair, agony, and pain grows wisdom. Therefore, emotions can create overwhelming sorrow while experiencing such calamities until it becomes almost impossible for anyone other than the recipient to understand or relieve the anguish of another. The event itself is a process, and like most processes, they take time. I can recall years back, while living in Colorado, when my next-door neighbor's new home burned to the ground on a cold Christmas Eve, destroying everything in it.

Nothing was left, not family pictures, heirlooms, or prized possessions. Nothing could be salvaged. Everything they owned was destroyed. Now, imagine coming home and seeing all you've worked for being destroyed right before your eyes, and there is nothing you can do to save it. Regardless of the depth of their friendships and closeness to the community, there was no amount of comforting, support, consoling, or even money that could make this family feel there was a purpose to this act. In fact, they questioned God as to why He allowed this to happen. It was only through the process of grieving, and a long painful journey of recovery did things get better, and even years later, scars still remained from the event.

Pain and a realization of any experience always has to run their course before healing occurs. After the event, you still may require time to come to terms with your new life. The night before Jacob and I left the amusement park we stopped to report his lost hat at the security office. As we waited to speak with the officer, others who had lost important items were in various lines. You could see the pain of loss on their faces. Whether a wallet, car keys, glasses, or even hats, each item lost was essential to its owner. Some knew where they had lost their possession, while others did not.

Along with their adversity, these events are custom-made just for the individual. Just as in life, there are times when we know of the small, seemingly insignificant ingredients that contribute to our loss. Deep down, we may even see the tragedy as part of our own doing. While there are other times when we did not see the event coming, nor could we figure out why we were divinely chosen to experience it. When we become aware of our own mistakes, hindsight becomes 20/20.

Another important lesson I learned from this is that your challenge is to walk away and leave it alone once you have done your best. I know it sounds strange, but it takes a disciplined person to do that. In other words, leave the issue alone, go about life doing other things, and watch what happens. As adults, our problem is it sometimes becomes impossible for us to leave 'the thing' alone.

We agonize, rationalize, strategize, suffer from guilt, get angry, and keep tinkering with it. All these actions ultimately allow more emotional entanglements to occur, often getting the best of us. Sometimes we get in our own way. After experiencing catastrophic events, getting on with life can be difficult until the pain subsides and healing occurs. Another painful but necessary lesson I learned from *The Hat* was how to get out of my own way, so I did not block the process that allowed blessings to flow to me.

In Jacob's case, once leaving the Lost and Found office that night, we did everything to provide the officer with the appropriate information to make it easier to locate the hat. What's interesting is upon calling the security officer to check on Jacob's hat, the officer responded with something that still brings goosebumps to my arms. She said that what helped us get the hat back so quickly and worked in our favor was that Jacob's hat already had his name in it. To me, that was powerful! I was stunned. Not because his mom wrote his name inside the cap (which was a great idea), but because I had fallen from grace. I had lost my hat; my income, status, and life as I once knew it, and my ego suit had now been shredded into a million pieces. I had lost my things, my stuff, and I wanted it back. And that's when I finally got it! It finally clicked.

The truth was that everything I thought I had lost already had my name on it, so in reality, at some point, it had to come back to me. I just had to have the necessary faith to believe it would return. I had to exhibit a childlike attitude of faith. Be blind for a while. After all, how much of my old stuff was necessary anyway, or was it just that my ego and pride had taken such a beating I needed the stuff to let others know I was still in the game.

Once Jacob and I returned home that evening from Six Flags, he did not fret over his hat. He went to bed and left it alone. The next day, he went about his childlike business as he usually did, just doing what kids do. Even though his hat was miles away with the possibility of never returning, it miraculously made its way back home without him ever knowing the mechanics of 'how.' Wow! It was then that I truly understood the magnitude and power of faith. Faith provided me with the energy that made the universe respond. Faith, combined with favor, allows God to move on your behalf to restore and far exceed the value of anything you lost.

I have learned that God challenges us through adversity and gives us another chance at a new life through those events. Our lives are being reinvented and refined in the furnace of adversity. For many of us, it is not basking in the blessing we fear; we enjoy that, but again, we despise the process. Remember this, when involuntarily growth is scheduled, based on our destiny; our old stuff cannot come with us; especially when the acquisition of our 'things' was built on dishonesty, false pride, or any other unstable foundation. They must be released. For me, this lesson was incredibly sobering because I spent endless nights crying, going in and out of various states of depression, even thoughts of suicide.

After such a loss, I believed my reason for living was over. In reality, my new life had just begun, and I had no idea. The question most of us spend time repeatedly asking ourselves is 'why?' Why me? Why did this happen, and why didn't it happen to someone else? The next question that consistently plagues us is, 'how?' How can I come back from this event? How can I get my stuff back? How will things work like before? How can God restore me to a better position than before?

Even after I took that hard look at my situation and knew some of the answers, I still spent many sleepless and agonizing nights trying to figure out the answers. From the time we arrive on Earth, growth is continual and expected. Growth continues from infancy to adulthood, including mind, body, and spirit. However, to grow means we must also shed or let go of some things to gain new ones. An infant cannot remain a baby. By default, it continues to evolve into adulthood. Nothing remains the same forever. If your stuff' is genuinely yours and already has your name on it, just like Jacob's hat, it will always find its way back to you in one form or another.

Just as I explained to Jacob at the amusement park, "Just because you don't win a prize today doesn't mean you're not a winner. But what happens when you do win is that the winning is usually bigger, better, and sweeter than anything you could have ever won before. The final reward will be better than all the other stuff you've missed combined." Oh, and that family in Colorado, not only did the event bring the family closer, but they rebuilt their house with all new furnishings and with more upgrades than they previously had.

Now, as an adult whose life was once obliterated into a million pieces, I realize this statement may fall on deaf ears; however, once you break through the brick wall of realization, you will find there is truth buried behind it. It's just the way the universe works. Just as Jacob's hat came back to him, so shall yours. Mine did. So, in the meantime, during those dark and uncertain days, weeks, months, or even years, what will you do while you wait on your hat?"

"When the darkness of the abyss surrounds you, the voice of a true friend is like a life preserver thrown to a drowning man."
                    Steven LeMons

"*The thing about walking on water,
is what happens once you realize
you're doing it.*"

Steven LeMons

Dear Heavenly Father, instead of a verbal prayer, today I come before you compelled to write these words as my way of expression, instead of getting on my knees. Regardless of the method I choose to reach you, I know you will always hear and not judge me. To you, how I reach you is not as important as the fact that I make the effort.

I would first like to thank you for sustaining my life, sharing with me, taking care of me, protecting me, feeding me, growing me, stretching me, and unconditionally loving my resistant spirit. No one loves me as you do or who can lovingly express their acceptance of me, regardless of my imperfections or crimes I have committed against you. For it has always been your unconditional love and forgiveness that has granted me grace, mercy, and favor.

You have a greater love for me that is deeper than the love I have for myself. After all, I do not honestly know how to love myself or anyone, for I am incredibly flawed and imperfect. I am constantly in pursuit of the flesh and my own way.

Realizing this, my lack of knowledge lines my path to self-destruction. For it is my 'not-knowing' that allows me to realize just how much I do not know. At this stage of life, I find it hard to express the very thing my heart desires, which is to love and be loved. But I know that you do, and you can give me the words to express myself. The truth is, it's not as easy as one might think. But it is your love that surpasses all time and space. Your love is more profound than a mother's love and all-encompassing. It is the love of a maker's spirit. It is universal and omnipotent. It is the love you died for.

With all the love you possess for me as my creator and lover of my soul, why is it that I still despair? Why is my heart so heavy? Why do I feel so worthless, discouraged, and so heavy in spirit? Is it because I have never learned the actual reality of acceptance? Is it that somewhere in the growing stages that I am now reaping the consequences from the simple lessons about accepting myself, loving myself, or being more confident in myself? Are these steps that I have failed to learn fundamental to my emotional and spiritual success? Why is it that regardless of how many mountains I climb, records I set, or achievements I accomplish, I still feel like a failure and do not realize my true value? Why Lord, why?

It is the day before my birthday. I know it should be a happy time, yet I find myself tired, longing for human touch and validation from you. Is it normal for one to feel such despair right before such a significant milestone? It is hard for me to accept my arrival at this new place in life where the outward manifestation of my inner accomplishment does not seem to be in sync with each other.

I would like to know that this treacherous and seemingly endless journey does have a purpose, one that has a blessed and joyous meaning far beyond anything I can imagine or envision. From the outside looking in, others think I should be grateful. I am attractive and blessed, in good health, and physically fit, can still think with fantastic clarity; I am creative and gifted with extraordinary talent blessed by God, yet why don't I feel like I am winning? I would like to believe that in my life, not only does the journey matter but so do I. If so, why then does such heaviness weigh me down?

With all my blessings, something essential seems to be missing. Somewhere there is an imbalance.

I can feel something is missing amongst all Stevens' confetti parades and 'atta-boys'. I just cannot seem to find the missing link. Is it mental, emotional, or just imaginary? Or am I overlooking a missing spiritual element so fundamental to the manifestation of my inner success until I find myself repeating many of the same situations, i.e., adversities for lack of this golden serum or critical principle? Until I realize what it is, I find myself like a hamster on a treadmill, expending energy but going nowhere. I have everything I need to ride the winds of success, yet why do I keep falling short of the correct implementation or application strategy required to bear the right fruit?

When it's all said and done, could the missing ingredient be just time? It has been said that "All things happen in their own time," right? I don't know, but it appears that time is passing me by, so whatever the missing ingredient is in my life, I am burdened and tormented by the lack of it. Some say, "Steven, don't try to figure this thing out, just let it be. Just let go and let God. He reveals everything in His time. Just get on with your life." Or, "You overthink. Just give it a rest. Let it take care of itself." Even though some of what they say may sound like worn-out clichés, there may be some degree of truth in them.

I believe God has provided man with something unique that He did not intend for animals. He has given us free will. He has given us the power to think and make choices, including serving Him, that allows us a better quality of life than the animals. The Lord doesn't make us serve him; we choose to; the problem is, He has generally chosen you first and did not inform you about His decision. If that's the case, you will know sooner than you think.

For example, if you're a rabbit or lion, you're either predator or prey. Although some would argue that humans never have to choose whether to be predator or prey because we are allowed free will; therefore, we can independently select our path to whatever direction we desire. Consequently, we usually don't have to worry about being eaten by a lion or cannibal when we get up in the morning. Unlike the poor rabbit, we have choices.

My choice is to understand. Not just to be a passive participant sitting on the sidelines observing my life passing before me, void of insight, but be an active participant in it. My choice is to understand the why's of my journey, rather than quietly and unknowingly march to life's gas chamber or open the treasure chest without ever knowing or understanding what's inside it.

To some, this may sound confusing. However, when successfully moving through life, one must look at every aspect of their existence, not just live life with their head in the clouds or the sand, but address reality with curiosity, desire, and boldness, not just with fear and trembling. We must also learn to recognize and understand our feelings. Doing so allows us greater insight into who we are and how to manage our emotions. Not acknowledging one's feelings becomes a set-up for things to come, and it's usually not good.

Acknowledgment of guilt, pain, insecurities, resentment and any other thoughts you hold against yourself or others is significant in limiting one's growth. Letting go of negative emotions against others allows you freedom from expending harmful energy and promotes your growth and forward movement. Is there someone you know who requires your forgiveness, but you haven't? Think it through, and afterward, you'll find that now is a good time for making an effort. You may also have to forgive yourself.

In my attempts at rationalizing this life-riddle, I have often grappled with aspects of my existence. I am open to both the positive (stuff I uncover about myself I like and that makes me feel good) and negative information (things I am not so proud of that frightens me). In so doing, I lay my soul bare.

Why not come clean? It makes no sense to lie to yourself. Lying works to prolong your progress and suffocates growth. Being honest with yourself, no topic in your life is off-limits, nor should any stone be left unturned. Dishonesty or ego has no place in a truthful self-assessment, even with the stuff you take to the grave with you. It is about searching the deepest and darkest corners of your soul to find the truth to what you are seeking. It won't be pretty, but you will better understand the person staring back at you in the mirror.

Reflecting on past experiences, I can see myself as a young child, about seven or eight, contemplating. During one of these such contemplations, I asked myself, "What happened to that little boy who just wanted to do something special? The little kid who just wanted to fly airplanes, fall in love, stay married to the love of his life, and inspire others?" As my life played before me like a feature film, I saw one filled with fear, poverty, abuse, pain, guilt, lack of knowledge, ignorance, missed opportunities, and devastating regret. Like a runaway train, I saw a life that at some point had derailed and could not get back on track.

I have also come to see and know the strong man who lives inside me, one who is incredibly passionate and persevered. A man who is resilient, accomplished, possesses strong character and courage. This man loves and possesses an overwhelming desire to help others improve the quality of their own lives. I have come to know that I am a strong and uniquely beautiful person, yet my two lives are in direct conflict with each other to claim the territory within me. If we are honest with ourselves, many of us experience similar challenges. The struggle is usually ongoing and can last years. The key is not to allow our carnal side to break us down and win.

Looking back, maybe my impending birthday is getting the best of me. Perhaps I struggle with myself for not reaching the academic or professional milestones I had envisioned by this age, or maybe I fell short of reaching the financial goals I forgot to set for myself. Isn't it funny how we become guilty and insecure of judging ourselves through the standards of others? For me, a birthday is a time marker that visually and psychologically reminds me more of what I have not accomplished than what I have.

At this juncture, I am in a significant transition and I feel out of control. Almost everything I once considered valuable had been taken away on this journey. My life is under construction, or should I say reconstruction, where the rules of engagement are re-written. Time, as I once knew it, has been destroyed and re-calibrated. I am trying to believe that could be a good thing.

I currently find myself starting over, living over, and approaching life from an entirely different perspective. And although I have paid a heavy price for the fruits of earning this wisdom, at this phase of life, my ultimate fear is that I may have missed my calling for using this wisdom.

I feel as though I have been marking time in another dimension instead of this one. It is another circle of life I have yet to experience. Have I always worked, strived, achieved, given, and become wiser, yet labored in a dry wasteland where nothing ever seems to grow? Like some black and white Twilight Zone television episode where things never bear fruit regardless of what the farmer does, I feel I have labored in a dimension where the land is barren, and adversity forever reigns.

Right now, time is positioning itself to become more and more the enemy. For me, the clock of yield is ticking ever louder. I can hear its relentless tick-tocks over and over again. Once abundantly producing the juicy and luscious fruits of my labor, my fields have now dried up, and although still empty, I cannot plant enough seed to grow before another dust storm looms on the horizon. I now feel stalked by uncertainty; shame is my reality, and loneliness is my companion. The fear of my uncertainty has become my hunter, and I have become its prey. Like the rabbit and the lion, prey or predator, it is now me, the cornered rabbit who fears being devoured.

I am disappointed at what has now become of my choices. I am sinking in the quicksand of an unfulfilled life, trapped in a perpetual cycle of nothingness, trying with everything inside me to escape from a centrifuge of adversity where I continually repeat the same failures. My personal goal is growth, not to turn a blind eye to my own shortcomings; instead, I acknowledge and accept them. This way, my flaws have less power over me. Please, Lord, free me through your terrific favor, so I see myself for who I truly am and my capabilities. I may not deserve it, have earned it, or have paid the price for it, but I humbly beg you.

I realize I can never be good enough to earn your favor, yet I desire it. I also realize its value and power and know what I can do with it. I understand its impact on others and myself. I am not unaware of the responsibility that comes with the power of being chosen. Although I am far from perfect or deserving, I realize the responsibility of being chosen by you. However, that's another story. I believe there has to be active favor going on in my life. My difficulties are not going to go in vain. There has to be a reason and purpose for all this. There has to be a reason for my existence. If I am your chosen, then show me. No, I am not a 'Doubting Thomas,' well, maybe a little, but in my heart and soul, I would just like to know, what do you want me to do?

I claim the renewing of my mind through your spirit. I know you can reach me wherever I am. Knowing this, I should be happy. Even though I am aware that there is a process for everything, why do I still feel so alone? As the fragility of being human is realized, and although I know and appreciate the outcome, which is the acquisition of wisdom; however, I still despise the process. Due to its weight, I have grown weary of it, of going through turmoil over and over. In the mornings, my bones creak under the heaviness and mental weight of unfulfilled dreams. The pains associated with human fermentation have begun to take their toll, and yet, in my life, the sun has still to rise. I remain in darkness, with no daylight on the horizon.

It is unwise for me to love you for only personal gain. You are not the God of my heavenly ATM; only there for me to send up a short order prayer just to get a need met or dial up a blessing order for express pickup like ordering a pizza. I am called to love you simply for who you are. You are my God, my hope, my spiritual comforter, and my provider. You are all things to me and more. Although my mind realizes these facts, my heart still breaks. I return to the question, "Why am I so broken?" My soul and spirit feel broken, warped from their original shape—disfigured, stretched, and shattered.

Maybe that is only how I see myself, but not how You see me. Is it just that I am human and flawed? A part of myself loves me, believes in me, and encourages me. In contrast, the other side of me sees himself as a dissatisfied failure, who has left a trail of carnage and desolation throughout his battered and bruised life. I am not worthy. I am torn—double-minded, full of iniquity.

Like a car with the gear selector in drive, while at the same time having a foot on the brake, I make no forward progress —again, I am torn. Maybe this has just become a way of protecting myself; if I see myself as unworthy, I become unworthy. This way, I am not disappointed if I don't achieve anything.

Regardless, after surviving the process, when all is all said and done, I will bask in the knowledge that my best days are not behind me but ahead. Therefore, I will not align myself to negative and self-defeating thoughts, even though it becomes easier to allow them to take root. These thoughts grow in barren land and become the seeds of destruction. Sometimes the idle mind is not only the devil's playground but becomes fertile ground for self-defeating seeds to take root.

Once they take hold of the mind, they grow into a mindset that makes breaking free from self-destructive thoughts and behaviors difficult. Although I struggle, in my heart, I know, with Christ's love, I will not just survive but thrive. By nurturing a healthy relationship with God, I am provided fertile spiritual ground for producing the visible and tangible fruit that manifests itself due to my labor. I must believe this.

Beyond the shadow of any doubt, I am a success and more than a conqueror.

*"Even in the darkest of night
if you look for it, there will always
be a bright spot somewhere."*
Steven LeMons

Part IV.

Empowerment

Empowerment is the gift to a broken spirit that has the courage and the will to survive and overcome in the mist of adversity.

As life challenges seize upon our imagined reality, many of us slowly give way to the consequences of our experiences by letting go of the dreams we once held fast. When we do, a part of us dies.

Dreams

During childhood, many of us entertained healthy dreams. Most of us remembered being asked the question, "What would you like to be when you grow up?" The typical response was usually: a doctor, lawyer, football player, nurse, astronaut, or a host of other wildly imaginative choices. Sometimes, if we let our imagination run wild, we would even combine multiple careers so diverse we could not accomplish them all in three lifetimes, but at least we dreamed. We also believed we could become anything, have anything, and do anything our hearts desired. The confines of reality did not restrict our dreams; therefore, anything was possible.

But for some, age brought realizations that becoming a pilot, doctor, and professional athlete all simultaneously was more challenging than we expected; so, many slowly gave way to the consequences of their experiences and let go of the dreams they once held close. We let go of our beliefs and our childhood vision of possibilities. When we did, part of us died.

Over the years, as we experienced the untimeliness of an unexpected pregnancy, domestic abuse, drug addiction, cancer, poverty, or the unexpected loss of employment, somehow, we destroyed our ability to dream. Dreaming appeared insignificant, and there were more important priorities, such as getting on with life. Interestingly, experiences in our lives some may have viewed as impossible became the motivation for others to achieve their dreams. Why? Because they refused to allow their dreams to die.

They also remained steadfast in their desire to achieve them. I will refer to a young man named James, who shared part of his story with me and revealed that his dreams had died at one time. James stated that his dreams were so far from his present reality that he had long since quit imagining himself ever becoming anything, let alone successful. The challenges he faced battling drugs, multiple incarcerations, and generational poverty worked against him. He said his life experiences had virtually destroyed his ability to believe in himself or any dream he had.

Not only had he lost his ability to dream, but he also resented anyone who dared attempt to resurrect them. About six months later, fate uniquely aligned with James. He experienced a life-changing circumstance when he met an individual who would help him transform his thinking and life forever. In short, fate placed James in a position where his path intersected with someone who soon became his mentor, not someone trying to convince him to dream, but who saw in him value he could not see in himself.

James was empowered to reconnect with something deep beneath the surface of his life he needed to see, which was critical to his transformation. By reconnecting with himself, James jump-started his dreams. Through this chance meeting and relationship, James regained his ability to dream and with help from other mentors, transformed his thinking. James is now a successful college graduate and a mentor to others.

Do you think this story is unusual? For some, maybe. For others, it could be an example of what it takes to reignite the dreamer in themselves. What about you? James' story could be the catalyst that could guide you to reassess your own value and worth. It could be just what you need to get off the couch of "I'll do it someday," or "I'll get around to it," to doing it right now. However, our dreams may sometimes seem nonexistent, somewhere inside of ourselves lying beneath the rubble of broken promises, numerous failures, and disappointments, our dreams, although faint, still live.

Even though there was just a sliver of hope, he still held onto his dream of attending and graduating from college at James' core. Maybe you haven't given up on making your dream to graduate college, travel the world, write a book, or own a business, a reality. If so, don't stop; take action. What do you want to do, achieve, and leave as part of your legacy? Your commitment requires much more than just saying you want to achieve something; it demands work, drive, purpose, a time investment, and an insatiable desire to move beyond your current set of circumstances.

Sir Isaac Newton's third law describes it best; "For every action, there is an equal and opposite reaction." Simply put, you must invest something in yourself to reap meaningful results. Doing this means applying effort as never before and learning from others who are reaching goals you would like to achieve. They can even offer meaningful advice for helping you live your best life.

You encounter people who have overcome many of the same obstacles and challenges you may be facing. Once you become aware of their presence, go past your fear or ego and reach out. Begin setting realistic goals and follow through on them, whether to find a mentor, devote time to sharpening your goals, or revising your resume. If your goal is to become an astronaut, but you hate math, your chances of fulfilling that dream are almost nonexistent. And if you say you'd like to become an attorney, yet you hate reading because you think it's boring, you may as well kiss that career choice goodbye. It's just not realistic. My question is not what you would like to become, but is your desire strong enough to power that dream to become a reality?

Regardless of circumstances, an obsession for success must exist and eclipse any difficulty or obstacle it encounters for dreams to become a reality. The individual has to be moved beyond the temporary discomfort of any negative reality to embrace the accomplishment of a larger dream. They must be willing to propel themselves beyond excuses, procrastination, late or incomplete paperwork, or missed opportunities. They must burn with a dream that consumes them. Showing up late or maintaining an unpleasant attitude could be keeping you from achieving your ultimate desires.

Your dream must serve as the driving force in your life. It must be a catalyst for transformation beyond merely hoping for success to create it. As a rocket blast free of Earth's gravitational pull, so must the desire to achieve your dream from anything attempting to diminish its power, kill or even steal your dream. You must train your mind to recognize and seize opportunities that move you closer to your achievement.

Dreams worth dreaming are worth achieving. Like so many others who started with enough hope to build a fulfilling life but lacked forward motion, my challenge to you is to act and not allow your dreams to die. Regardless of whether anyone else believes in them or not, the most important thing is that you believe in them and yourself. Whatever challenge you may be facing, know that this too shall pass. If you remain strong, your challenge will not break you but make you stronger. So, hold fast to your dream as if it were a winning lottery ticket because it just may be your winning ticket to an incredible life.

Never give up on your dream; live it and re-dream it every day. If James can do it, you may be able to do it too.

WHO

Who Got Game?

A movie by film director Spike Lee stars Denzel Washington as a lifetime prisoner tricked into getting his son to sign up to play basketball for the warden's college alma mater. The problem is two-fold; Denzel has a not-so-good relationship with his son, which he would like to change, and a dishonest warden, who once he gets what he wants, will not keep his end of the bargain. The title of the movie is "Who Got Game?"

What usually comes to mind when you hear someone use the phrase "who got game"? Is it referring to someone who knocks the cover off the ball each time they step up to bat? Or is it someone surrounded by those who set and achieve goals, drive fancy cars, live in big houses, make financial noise, and by that default, becomes one who has game? In either case, my question is, do you have game?

Do you have what it takes to make a deal and win with yourself? Can you throw down and orchestrate a transaction that increases your ultimate net worth beyond your self-inflicted verbal propaganda? "Let's Make A Deal" I'm Monty Hall, and you've chosen 'what's behind door number two?' You've won the shortcuts of life; the instantaneous feel good quick-results money and all the perceived trappings associated with the high-life. Do you quit school, get a job, take the fast cash? Or do you trade it for the hard work and the surprise waiting for you behind door number three?

Oops, you picked a long-term commitment. You've got to take the high road, set realistic goals, and stay focused on achieving them for longer than a year. Your prize, long-term success. Are you up to the challenge, or will you take the money and run? That's what I thought. Do you really believe that winning millions of dollars in the lottery will solve all your problems, your failed marriages, your non-functional relationship with your children, or even your financial situation? Do you believe ten million dollars can cure your lack of ambition or confidence in yourself?

Can that same ten-million-dollar loaded gun change your small-minded mentality, fear of success, or the failure mindset that's haunted you all your life? So, do you have game, or does the game got you? If you've got it, call next up!

So, waiting on your turn, let's think about what someone who does have game looks like. It is someone who's got their act together in such a way that when they walk down the streets and into an arena, it makes the crowd roar and women squeal because they know who entered the room. Instead of wanting to be like Mike, they all want to be like you; walking in your suede shoes, driving your red supercar, having the multiple digits in your bank account, living in your house, and sleeping in your king-size Sealy Posturepedic bed, maybe even with you. Oh man, it must be nice to have some game!

Having game is the person who actually does walk away with Park Ave, Boardwalk, Marvin's Garden, the most toys, the girl or guy, and all the dead presidents too? Having game is standing up and fighting one more time for what you believe in, even after adversity says, "there's nothing left, lights out, game over, let it go," but your attitude refuses to let it die. You stand once more, like a second effort hit by Emmitt Smith, a 40-foot Tiger Woods putt in the last round of the Masters, or the devastation of a Serena Williams opponent at Wimbledon. Is that how you play?

If yes, then you have some serious game. Nike says, *"Just do it,"* but Gatorade asks, *"Is it in you?"* Is it? Ask yourself. Having game is setting goals and getting things done with a sense of urgency. It's focusing on the real, avoiding the bullshit, and not allocating time to time-wasters. Having game means possessing the desire and passion for winning without compromising buying into unfavorable circumstances. It means getting up after being knocked down, not just once, but as many times as it takes until you win. It's realizing that winning is a process, which can be challenging but necessary. People with game understand failing provides examples of how not to do something; failure provides a perspective success does not.

It's all part of the game, and if you got game, you get it. Having game means you become the brand that develops a frequently imitated style that can never truly be duplicated. It is a one and only, an original. It possesses a flavor all its own. It means having the street flava of Jay Z, the analytical skills of a Bill Gates, the swagger and mindset of Barack Obama, and dollars of Sir. Richard Branson. Rolling down the street in your red Bugatti, pumping Michael Jackson tunes on the Bose while popping Skittles, puts you squarely in the game, but ain't nobody's business but mine and my baby's—cause you are the "thriller," and you got game.

You got game when you make the play continue until you say "lights out". It continues until you decide when the game is over, when you get the last lick, when you pass, go and collect 200.00 dollars, and when the lady with the big voice finally does sing. You got game when you can call the hard shots and be willing to take the hits, live with the accountability and responsibility of failing or winning, and do it all without making excuses.

You got game when you can point the ship of your mind and focus in any direction, and despite how dark or rough the seas are, you know that through it all, there's a beautiful beach somewhere with a reserved spot for your butt-print. You got game when you are willing to stand for something; Black Lives Matter, White Lives Matter, All Lives Matter; speak your mind, drop the mic, and not be afraid to prove your point; that's the kick-ass joint. When you are willing to go the extra mile, not because it's popular or convenient, but because it's the right thing to do, you got butt-kicking game.

Waiting at the stop sign of life, when someone pulls up beside you, what will they see? Will they see a person driving a broken-down hooptie, smoking, in need of a mental, emotional, and spiritual tune-up? Will your hooptie vibrate relentlessly from the fear of "I don't have enough, it's somebody else's fault, they won't let me play, or I just can't hang's?" Or, will they look over, see you, do a double-take, and say, "Damn, that's who I wanna be like?" Will they see someone who is not only in the right ride but has the right stride and the proper glide? Will they see the big dog, the lead dog, the boss hog, the let's git it on King Kong player representing OG's that are bygone? Will they see the Stone Cold of the who got gamers, a future member of the gamers and baller hall of famer, a legacy maker, soul shaker, and adversity playmaker?

When they do pull up next to you at that stop sign, will they you or someone else with everything you could have had? I hope not.
Cause you got what everyone in America wants, what people in the world are dying to get, what some folks dream about, obsess about, but don't have the confidence or courage to work out. You have what is worth more than money, more than pure gold itself. You possess what no amount of money can buy, but with it, you can buy anything your heart desires; you got it, just know it, now flaunt it and dare to show it. You were born with it; you got game.

Life is your playing field, so get up, get out of bed, quit whining, complaining, and making excuses. Get off your ass, turn off the TV, get your head in the game, and play.

Stand Firm

We often find ourselves feeling lost, alone, and uncertain during times of extreme difficulty and challenge. Sometimes it's as though our prayers seem to fall into an empty void; we do not get an answer. We often feel as though we should just give up during such times. But what advice do you think God would give us? What do you think He would say? Would He tell us to give up? Or, be like a tree, and, "Stand Firm?"

I.

As Christians, we constantly face inner demons and our unique challenges. Even though we consider ourselves Christ-like, there are times when we all fall short, get tired, and often feel as though we cannot measure up to the Christ-like expectations we signed onto, let alone God's. We can and often do find ourselves asking the question, why? Why now, and why me?

As I struggled through various periods of on-again, off-again calamities I feared would never end, accompanied by endless days of confusion so challenging it was hard to know which way was up. I found some of the most straightforward decisions beyond my capability. As much as my vain attempt at facing challenges with courage and faith, I continuously questioned the tough calls and chaotic events happening in my life. On many occasions, I saw myself as a total wreck, yet I kept asking God, "What is truly going on in my life?"

We all knew that once we prayed the Sinner's Prayer and began our Christian walk, it would not be easy. We knew there would be lions and tigers and bears all along the way, just waiting to pounce. We also discovered that no one is immune to tests, trials, and times when we question whether or not praying that prayer was worth it. Armed with this knowledge, few of us had any idea our lives could be reduced to nothingness.

In my experience, I have discovered that during uncertain times, the enemy and his minions work overtime. Their diabolical powers and principalities in high places are always busy, making every effort to steal, kill, and destroy what joy and happiness you may possess. In fact, he desires to wreak havoc and kill every budding and purposeful fruit on our tree of life before it even begins to grow. His mission is to ultimately destroy every idea, dream, and gift God has given us, and he will stop at nothing before breaking your spirit and soul. Frankly, there is nothing or anyone in your life who is off-limits, not your mother, father, children, friends, teacher, pastor, or anyone else. Neither young nor old are excluded. Everyone is a potential target.

Whether your challenge revolves around keeping a spiritual covering over your household, protecting your health, career, finances, or managing the impact of a dysfunctional relationship that makes coming home difficult, all can test your spirituality, sexuality, or even have you questioning if there is a God. The enemy is masterful at exploiting the potential of a lie. Lies are the arrows shot from the bow of deceit. They form a narrative of 'doubt' to control and destroy their victim. Satan is the originator of lies and guardian of his post. He has dispatched an army of demons, hell-bent on doing their best to break you, bind your mind, destroy your God-given potential, and detach you from the love of Christ.

As much as I hate to admit it, there were times when I felt like I did not want to live. I wanted to die. Yes, there were times when living itself seemed like a burden. Blow-after-blow, endless stumbling blocks tried to convince me it would be better if I were not alive; after all, who would care. I reasoned that my family would be better off and more stable without me. Any dream of success I possessed was pushed further away from ever becoming a reality.

Even though I knew this was a lie of the enemy, I could not help but own it. I found the enemy used every avenue, opportunity, and unfair advantage to attack my family and me. My resistance was beaten down so much that I couldn't defend myself from its vicious blows. Whenever there seemed to be even a little bit of good news, another setback would rear its ugly head and strangle any shred of hope I held. This kept me in a pit of discouragement and despair. In fact, I found myself in a constant state of depression. I wanted to believe in the power of God, but yielding to the flesh and doing and not wanting to be in control.

There were days when just getting out of bed was a challenge. Every bone in my body creaked and ached under the tremendous weight and strain of the mental, emotional, and spiritual weight. It seemed that my head, eyes, back, and even feet were inwardly crying out in anguish as I faced each long, hard, disappointing day. At times, my body felt as if it could not support the stress, tension, frustration, and agony, any longer—at least not on this day. I pleaded. Where are you, Lord?

As someone who has always prided himself as a self-motivator and is not quick to complain, I experienced days when it seemed easier to get back into bed and pull the covers over my head. However, at the time, being a father and a husband who was fighting the demons of guilt and insecurity associated with being unemployed, somehow, I had to put on a positive demeanor and find the strength to keep moving forward, even though I didn't want to.

I knew others depended on me for solutions even though I had no answers myself. Who was I? Was I the magic man, the Great Black Hope, the Gung-Ho negro, who could always make something happen? Was I someone they could always count on to at the last minute to pull a rabbit out of my hat? This time, it wasn't working. I had a mile-long resume, yet I couldn't buy a job. So why not just go back to bed? Why not find something to help me ease the pain; a vice, an outside woman, drugs, alcohol, anything? The truth is, I couldn't even if I wanted to. I knew this was a spiritual battle, and it was much bigger than me.

Amid my tears, I constantly found myself asking, "How did I get here? What am I doing here? How do I get out of this? Lord, when will it be my time, my season to reap the harvest? Get double for my trouble? Or see the windows of heaven open up for me? Is this real, or is it some bull? How much more of this can I take? But pray as I might, the answers to my questions just went unanswered, nowhere to be found. In the wee hours of the morning, as I paced back and forth, I often found myself devoid of sleep. I wrestled with endless thoughts consuming every minute of my day.

As Christians, we are told that when facing adversity, call upon the name of Jesus, and He will answer you because sometimes He is all you have left. Although there is truth to this statement, it is essential to note that His timing is not always ours. Suffering may last for a day, month, or even years, but that could be only a blink of an eye to Him. He has, however, left us with a promise. His grace is sufficient for anything we face. So why didn't I feel this while getting the spiritual, emotional, and financial crap beaten out of me?

I tried creating an external distraction by watching mindless television programs. I medicated myself with projects I thought would help take me away from the static clutter that seemed to possess my thoughts. When nothing brought peace, I lay flat out on the floor in my bedroom closet, not knowing which way to turn, tears streaming down both sides of my cheeks, begging the Lord to take away the pain and change my situation. Change did not come regardless of my prayers, cries, moaning, and groaning. Only more of the same torment. Why Lord, why? Would it be better if I were not here? Would it be better if I were dead? What good am I to my family? What a mess I have made of my life. What a mess.

II.

God, oh God, I need you. I need you now. I need you in the midst of my life and my pain. I am beyond tired and at the end of my rope. What would you have me do? Have I not been faithful and loyal to you? Have I not been a good servant? Why do I feel that I have been on a one-way trip to hell without ever leaving Earth?

As your faithful servant, I ask, what is this all about? What did I do wrong to deserve such agony? What should I be doing that I am not? Lord, please guide me! I cannot bear the pain of this cross any longer. It is not that I don't believe in you or lack faith; it is not that I do not realize I am in your presence, it just sometimes feels as if you are nowhere to be found. It is in those times, when I feel alone. I am alone and tired.

Please, God, just move in my life. I know you're watching over me, but why do I feel your presence as void? I suffer from a spiritual blackness so thick I cannot see through it. I cannot hear nor feel you. Why oh Lord, why? Please open a door or a window so I can see some form of heaven. Throw me a heavenly crumb or something just to let me know you are still speaking to me.

I'm not asking for much; not a wish-list of items, or my heart's desire, just relief from the suffering, relief from this agony. I have lost so much; I have lost everything. My finances are a wreck; my personal life is in turmoil; I have no job, my credit is shot, my self-respect and dignity are non-existent. Each day, I find my health getting progressively worse under the strain of uncertainty. I know that I cannot do it on my own. I need you to take my hand and guide me.

Where are the lines drawn between what I can do, what I should do, what I need you to do, and what you expect from me? And then you said, "To whom much is given, much is required." So, what is required of me? I find this cross too hard to bear. I am done, Lord. I ache. My body is weary, weak, and wracked with pain. I do not want to go on. I am done.

By now, there aren't any more friends, family, or confidants who will listen or help.

I find that some events are designed especially for the person experiencing them. No one else is there who can or will go through it with you. When faced with life-threatening cancer, your entire circle of so-called friends may pray for and with you. They may come to the hospital and sit with you, bring flowers and cards, or even call you on the phone, but at the end of the day, it is you alone who must be pushed through the double doors and endure surgery—only you.

All I have is you, Father God. I am too strong to feel sorry for myself, yet too weak not to. Please do not look upon me with pity, Lord, but again, I ask the question, why do I feel so forsaken? Why? I need you, oh God. I need you now. Please release me, restore me, replenish my life with waters that flow from heaven. Let me be a blessing, the blessing to others you intend for me to be. Let me be the head and not the tail. Give me a new life, a wonderful and rewarding life. Grant me abundance right now, or at least a word, Lord, just a word. One word that could let me know that you are still here, listening to my pleas. Just one. Lord, just give me a word from your voice. Please, God, just a word. Just one single word.

III.

And God said, "Stand firm. In the midst of all your adversity, I say, stand firm. While in the midst of your tears, your fears, and your pain, stand firm. Though the winds of a darkened life may howl in the middle of the night and you cannot see the light of day, stand firm. Though loneliness has wrapped itself around you like the stench of death on an expiring corpse, continue to stand firm.

Know that I am God, and I will be with thee until the end. Know that when there is no one else on this Earth to comfort you, hold you, understand you, or be with you, I will. For it is I who made you and not yourself. For I know just how much you can and cannot bear. Know that there is no one greater than me, for I am the Alpha and the Omega, the beginning and the end. Know that I have predestined you from the womb for greatness; however, you must toil in labor and give birth to the purpose for which I have destined only you to fulfill.

Know that you have been fearfully and wondrously made, and I have plans for you that you know not, but in the end, you will understand why there was so much pain in the delivery of your exultation. I have made plans for your success and yours alone. Plans that will not only impact you but worlds beyond your wildest imagination. Know that there is only one you, and although there may be others who look like you and sound like you, there is only ONE YOU!

I have not promised you that life on this Earth would be easy. Your thoughts, your personality, your heart, your soul, your spirit, and your gifts are yours and yours alone. There will always be days on your journey when you feel I have left you alone and your life has passed. My child, you should know that there is no greater love than the love I have for you that I would lay down my life for yours.

For whosoever will believe in me shall not perish but have everlasting life. It is you I have chosen not only to be blessed with eternal life but to have it more openly, fully, completely, and abundantly. I am abundance. I am life. I am God, and there is none other before me. Know that I am the great I AM, and nothing can separate you from my love.

I say unto you, for I am sure that neither death nor life, nor angels nor rulers, nor things present nor things to come, nor powers, nor height nor depth, nor anything else in all creation, will be able to separate you from the love of God in Christ Jesus our Lord. Have I forsaken thee? No. For I have chosen you to be like me, Christ-like. Therefore, you must endure the pain and humiliation of crucifixion just as I. But like me, you will rise again. For it is I who will raise you as a new creature for my purpose and for all to see.

You will be transformed and made whole. Instead, you focus on your emotions and the temporary pain associated with your calling. It is you who focuses on your dwelling place, your bills, your reputation, your pride, your wants, and needs, as well as what in life you believe you have missed and what you do not have, versus what I see in you, your purpose, and where I want you to be. It has already. It is predestined.

Your credit score does not define you, the car you drive, the house or sub-division you live in, the job title you have, the clothes you wear, your status, paycheck, or how much you have or do not have in comparison to others, for I have given thee the power to generate wealth. In my plan, I can give, and I can take away. It is not about things but about me. It is not about your pain but your purpose. It is not about the present circumstances but the spiritual presence of the anointing I have placed on your life, and it shall come to pass.

My promises are genuine, and my word is life. I have made you wealthy beyond anything you can comprehend. You have been given wealth from the inside out and not from the outside in. My wealth has no boundaries. The external will manifest in due time. But for now, I will provide.

Everything happens in its time, and everything for a reason; for a more extraordinary work is at hand that is bigger than you and more than you know. I have the power to allow you to be broken and shattered into a million pieces today and a multi-millionaire tomorrow. It is not about you having the things of this world; it is about the things of this world having you. There will be no pain or sorrow when I deliver you, but you shall cry only tears of joy. You will be wrapped, draped, and clothed, in the fullness of my love, my anointing, my blessing, my favor, and everything that was taken, shall be restored with interest.

I will not only give you rest; I will raise you to rule like Joseph and Solomon. Make you a royalty like Ester. Restore you as I did Job and give you double for your trouble. Give you the keys to the kingdom as I did David, and bless you with the light of life as I did, Mary. I will fill your heart with a joy you cannot contain.

I will prepare a table for you in the presence of your enemies. I will anoint your head with oil. Your cup will run over. Surely goodness and mercy shall follow you all the days of your life, and you will dwell in my house forever—my house. You will shine with the light of the living God. Many will be attracted to you, for you will be a blessing to others and an ambassador for me. You will draw others closer to me by your presence and your words; the words I will give thee. The blessing I bestow upon you will not be yours alone but also for your children and your children's children.

For I love you as I love the church, for whom I gave my life. You are mine, bought with a price, and chosen for my purpose. For I am God, and besides me, there is none other. For the enemy is no match for me; he has already been defeated, both in heaven and hell. Stand firm, and know that victory is mine, sayeth the Lord.

Therefore, again, stand firm and know that I AM GOD; in the face of illness, I AM GOD, in the face of adversity I AM GOD, in the divorce court I AM GOD, in your loneliness and despair I AM GOD, and when staring death in the face I AM STILL GOD. Stand firm, and know that the battle is not yours; it is mine. Stand firm and know that I am God, and besides me, there is none other. Stand firm, for I am with thee, and I am with thee always; until the end of time."

"Put on the whole armor of God, that ye may be able to stand against the wiles of the devil. For we wrestle not against flesh and blood, but against principalities, against powers, against the rulers of the darkness of this world, and against spiritual wickedness in high places."

Ephesians 6:11-12

Stand firm.

The
Aftermath

Whenever we experience catastrophic events or natural disasters such as hurricanes, tornados, or earthquakes, there is always a conclusion. It is known as "the aftermath." Webster's Dictionary describes aftermath as "the period immediately following a usually ruinous event." As you finally awaken from the stupor of your previous life and assess the devastation around you, there is usually an uncanny calm that captures the surreal appearance of what once used to be. What now lies in front of you was not what was there before. Regardless of its appearance, in the beginning, nothing appears the same. The location of homes, roads, barns, and cars is different from before. Everything has changed. Such is the case with ourselves. Once we face adversity victoriously, we are forever changed. We are stretched, growing personally, spiritually, and emotionally in ways we never imagined. We grow far beyond what we thought were our limits, yet just as the surrounding landscape, we also display the scars of change.

The storm's aftermath leaves the landscape and the people who survive the event different from when they first entered it. No longer is there a tendency to take others and life for granted. There is a profound appreciation for life and the simple things that are a part of it. A storm can truly devastate everything you had previously known or bring you closer to the people and things of importance if you allow it. The aftermath commands you to reassess your priorities and challenges you to look at everything differently, including yourself. Storms and their aftermath provide the adversity needed to create 'defining moments' that either catapult us into a whole new level of 'abundant life' or shatter the false securities we have built our monuments of pretense on. Monuments so fragile until once destroyed, we are usually ill-equipped to handle the seemingly endless onslaught of brokenness and devastation resulting from the experience. Through a deep love, trust in Jesus Christ, and our undying faith make survival and recovery possible.

A New You

It is now official. From the ashes of your past rises a new and more incredible you. You have come through the valley of the shadow of death, fought demons, slain dragons, and risen from what your enemies considered ashes. God has granted you a second or even a third opportunity to do more, become more, and live more. Yes, you will have scars; we all do. Scars remind us of where we've been and what we've been through. That nasty divorce, the bankruptcy, the embarrassment of losing your stuff, the death of your child, the sexual dysfunction and abuse you've dealt with throughout your life leaves reminders that you've been through something no one desires ever to experience

So, what will you do with this new life? What will it look and feel like? How will you act? I grew up listening to Michael Jackson on the radio. When President Kennedy was assassinated, I knew where I was. I grew up watching a dimly lit oval-shaped black and white television when only three television networks, NBC, ABC & CBS, existed. I now watch television programs on a 70' high-definition flat-screen television with surround sound speaker systems with the capacity of hundred more channels.

Advances in technology make it possible to bring the world into our living rooms or, for that matter, even our phones. Today, fifty years old is the new thirty, and thirty, the new twenty. So, with everything possible to make a new and exciting life, you've been reborn, so what will you do with your gifts, talent, abilities, looks, and health? God has blessed you with another chance to get it right, make a difference, and execute His legacy for your life. To activate this new life, it is up to you to plug into it and commit yourself to something bigger than yourself.

Set goals to improve your physical, emotional, and spiritual well-being. Get up, stop whining, do something different, change something, pursue some super realistic goal, volunteer, empower others, lose weight, quit smoking, increase your income, or break away from others who bring down your life.

You did not come through the adversity to accept the blessing and run the other way. Remember, God is too big for that. If you tuck tail and run the other way as Jonah did, He will find you regardless of where you go. Repeating the process is no fun. It's okay not knowing what to do or what God wants from you; however, during quiet reflection, seek him to uncover what He expects from you and what He wants to do for you. Trust God's words, not just those placed in the Bible, but the ones He has quietly placed in your spirit. Ask him, "What am I going to do with the rest of my life? If you seek Him, he will ultimately reveal it to you.

One thing is for sure, regardless of where life takes you, even on the journey of a lifetime, when you arrive at the hotel, unpack your bags, and look in the mirror, the reflection staring back at you will be that of your own. So, again, what will you do with your new life? Whatever it is, now is the perfect time to start. By its very nature, life is incredibly short. It is the canvas upon which we paint all our experiences. There is no telling where life can take us with effort, creativity, and God's favor. It is up to each of us to make the most of it.

However, without clear direction, excessive procrastination, unclear goals, a lack of accountability, and living under the delusion of having all the time in the world, we often rob ourselves of our best life. This places us in a position far worse than we previously experienced. It creates an unhappy string of unachieved goals rather than the successful outcomes God intends for us. If you have already reached the Promised Land, it is your responsibility to reach out and take it; this means pushing beyond self-imposed comfort levels that sometimes become our own worst enemy.

So, again, what will you do with your new life? If you allow it, time can become your worst enemy. As you seek God regarding your future, allow past experiences to be your stepping stones to incredible opportunities. Do not allow five, ten, or fifteen years of wasted time to lead you back to the exact situations where you find yourself asking the same question, "What am I going to do with the rest of my life?"

Consider this a new starting point and beginning that can provide you with the perfect opportunity for becoming a better husband, father, wife, mother, daughter, student, or whatever you choose. It is a brand-new day that you have never seen before, with all the blessings and benefits it has to offer. It is a unique opportunity for discovering a whole new you. So, kick up your heels, make a toast, and celebrate the incredible possibilities and opportunities God has in store for you. Give thanks to him, let go of your past, stay accountable, and make the best of your new life.

A New You

Open Doors

Throughout our lifetime, we will encounter challenges, many of which we may feel inadequately equipped to manage. During times when we've made unfavorable decisions, been falsely accused, find ourselves peering through the bars of a jail cell, in a hospital bed, standing in a food stamp line, or when our present reality doesn't align with anything we know, it forces us to ask the question, "how did I get here?" When we thought life couldn't get any worse, it did.

It was only a year, month, or even one week ago when your current set of circumstances seemed as far away from your life as the sun is from the Earth. The headlines you read about or heard in the news were about someone else, not you. Now, your current reality seems to have come out of nowhere, unexpected and unimaginable. Now, you're the front-page story instead of someone else. This 'thing' that has now come upon you seems hell-bent on destroying you and your family. Whatever the 'thing' is that's hell-bent on destroying you, it challenges everything inside, including your spirituality.

It brings you to your knees, making you cry out in pain to God, asking, "Lord, what now, why now, and why me?" In this collection of writings, conversations, prayers, and Godly arguments, I have shared insights from my personal experiences. I have allowed myself to be transparent and vulnerable, without pretense, laying bare the thoughts and emotions I felt as I experienced the painful process of what I saw as a form of crucifixion, resurrection, and refinement.

Although no two experiences are the same, we generally do not walk away from such encounters the same way as when we initially encountered them. Our lives genuinely become transformed. In the darkness and loneliness of transformation, I have discovered that I have committed acts to myself and others that I am not proud of. Sometimes I even questioned my integrity, motives, and actions. I realized that selfishness, ego, greed, and even vanity often drove my choices. However, at the time, had someone shared that truth with me, I would not have believed nor accepted it. Instead, perhaps, I would have mocked them.

Over time, I have learned, through painful lessons, that honesty is essential to the healing process. After all, lying to yourself and God about who you think you are only prolongs the process of suffering and the road to recovery. As for me, God already knew who I was. No one can hide their greed, lustful thoughts, deviant behaviors, gluttony, envy, anger, guilt, or other questionable acts from God; He already knows who you are.

With His help, I began to see my true self – in areas of greatness and weakness. I accepted those traits I am proud of and those needing improvement. Experiencing this didn't mean letting go of every flaw I had. I still struggle, but God already knows me and still loves me despite myself. Only by seeing ourselves for who we are, do we grow.

Our adversity presents us with a vehicle for change and growth. It acts as a catalyst for helping us achieve the life we are meant to live. Knowing ourselves enriches and adds value to our lives and fortifies our spiritual confidence. Think about it; God still chooses to use us despite our flaws. If He used people in the Bible regardless of their sins and weaknesses, why wouldn't He choose to use us? That would include you and me. That makes each of us unique.

There were times in my life when I would compare myself to others. Why? Because I did not realize my value. However, over time, I understood that those I compared myself to and my life with their purpose was different from mine. I realized that everyone on this Earth is on a different path and has a unique purpose. Imagine an interstate highway. Thousands of cars are going in the same direction, traveling to various destinations at different speeds. As individuals, we are similar. Although we may all be traveling on similar paths, our final destination may not be the same. However, many of us have no idea where we're going, what road we will take to get there, or what we'll do when we get to our destination.

Ultimately, it is God who directs our path. No two people are alike, and neither are their reasons for moving in the direction they are heading; therefore, comparing yourself, your talent, gifts, goals, appearance, wealth, and where you're heading with others is fruitless. Two people can have the same destination or goal in mind yet arrive at that destination or achieve that goal differently and at other times. Graduating from high school is a perfect example.

Three students graduating high school together may have a similar goal of graduating from college. The first student immediately enrolls in junior college. After two years, he receives an associate's degree. He is then awarded a scholarship to a local university, where two years later, he earns his bachelor's degree. His dream of graduating college is achieved in four years.

The second student is accepted and immediately enrolls into an out-of-state university. After two years, she believes that college is not for her, so she decides to quit school and enlist in the Air Force. After three years on active duty, she decides to become an officer; however, the career field she desires requires applicants to have a college degree. After five years, she enrolled in college to finish what she originally started. After seven years from her original plan, she finally completed her degree.

The third student decides to put off college for one year to save money and work full-time. However, due to a family crisis, that decision delays college – not for a year, but after marriage, a mortgage, raising three kids, and a full-time career. Therefore, after the children leave home and finances allow, this student attends and finally graduates college forty years later. Each student was on the same path, at the same time at one point, all with the same goal or destination in mind; that of graduating college at the same time. Although all achieved the goal or arrived at the destination, they arrived at different times.

Did they all succeed at achieving their goal? Yes. Did they arrive at the same time? No. Did they choose different directions to end up in other places? Yes. So, when it comes to destinations, realize that it is not necessary to compare yourself to others or feel as though you are not progressing because your path is different. Many of the goals and destinations someone else chooses may not suit you, or your plans may not be in their best interest. So, God grants us grace because we don't always make the right decisions. He fills in the gaps we cannot fill ourselves. He covers our mistakes and faulty decisions because he knows we are imperfect. This is why He died for us, to provide a covering we cannot provide for ourselves.

As you attempt to make sense of your own life, know that although I am not a psychiatrist or medical practitioner qualified to suggest how to live your life, I can offer some final thoughts and practical advice from my personal experiences. This information can be valuable to you on your journey, as it was to me during mine. Managing my adversities, I have discovered, or should I say uncovered, lessons and wisdom nuggets from others that have benefitted me greatly. I am humbled to pass along some of it to you in hopes that it provides comfort, inspiration, and encouragement during your challenging times.

Every word in this book describing the pain and emotions I express are not only genuine, but they have also allowed me to develop a degree of compassion for others I never thought possible. It has provided me with a better comprehension of what it feels like to walk in someone else's shoes. Learning how to separate my mind-clutter and recognize the voice of God in my life, I continued gaining a better understanding of His requirement of life.

As His voice becomes more apparent to me, I am charged with a better understanding of connecting with Him during the low times in my life. When I faced adversity that unexpectedly overtook my life, God shared His plan for my life that helped me navigate a successful outcome. I want to share a portion of it with you. Although based on my situation, you may apply much of this to yours. God does speak to us, and it is up to each of us to be sensitive and hear his voice and instructions. I sincerely hope these steps will benefit and impact your life as they have mine.

1. Receive the word.

Being sensitive, we allow ourselves to hear from God through prayer, fasting, and meditation. The Lord speaks to each of us in His own way, and when He does, you will know it's Him. He can also use multiple ways, not just one. Whether through a conversation with a stranger, a bible verse, television program, song, book, or spoken word, you can be moved by a word, message, or passage from the Bible your spirit will not be prepared or equipped to erase.

In John 10:27, Jesus said, "My sheep hear my voice, and I know them, and they follow me." This tells us that even though sheep are a metaphor, God does speak to us. In fact, He may give you a vision, verse, or word at the most unusual time. It could be a Bible verse you cannot forget or a comment that will not leave your thoughts. Pay close attention. It may not seem significant at the time, but know that later it will become crucial.

2. Look for the message in the word God is sharing with you.

God always has multiple reasons for doing something in your life. In the Bible, there are always instances where his decision to take action for or against one person impacted multitudes. In our lives, He never does something for just one reason or wastes opportunities of connecting with you. It's like trying to play chess with God. Before you've made the first move, He already has you in checkmate.

Remember, we can only see a small piece of the puzzle. He sees how we fit into His entire plan. In Jonah I: I, the very first chapter and verse, God said, "Now the word of the LORD came unto Jonah, the son of Amittai." The interesting thing about this verse is that the word of the Lord came to Jonah. First, it does not say Jonah went after it or even sought it out, but it came to him. Second, although Jonah was reluctant to God's request, he was the key to a bigger plan than he ever knew.

The truth is, many of us could not accept the plan God had for our lives even if revealed to us. Why? Because we most likely would see it as too big. We would look at ourselves as many of the servants God chose during biblical times and see our faults and flaws, not our strengths. "I can't write that well. I don't have the education. They won't listen to me. I don't have the money or resources. I can't speak to all those people," all would be our excuses for not rising to the challenge God would place before us.

Many of us believe people in the Bible were much more different than ourselves when they actually were not. These people were a collection of alcoholics, womanizers, prostitutes, thieves, prisoners, adulterers, murderers, and others suffering from illnesses and diseases. They were all people with flaws and infirmities, just like us. They were far from perfect, yet God still had conversations with them. He often spoke to them more than they wanted Him to, just as he does to us.

It is usually after the fact, or when we find our backs against the wall when we realize we already had the correct answer from the beginning but chose to go in a different direction. Just like Jonah, we do not have to chase God to hear his voice or discover what He wants us to do. In reality, He had already predestined us long before we ever knew what our true calling or purpose was, whether we accepted it or not.

We can always choose to run away, as did Jonah. But God ultimately has the last say. He always gets his man or woman; we just extend the time to complete the assignment. Eventually, the job will always be completed at the appropriate time. In the second verse, He gives Jonah a mission. "Arise, go to Nineveh, that great city, and cry against it, for their wickedness is come up before me." As we all know, Jonah did not want to go to Nineveh, nor did He want any part of that deal, so he rejected the assignment. Instead, Jonah went to Tarshish in an entirely different direction. When we do not listen to that voice of reason, which is the Lord, we often get ourselves into deeper trouble.

Remember when we talked about 'destinations?' Jonah never got to Tarshish, his destination. Instead, he ended up entangled in weeds in the belly of a whale. Remember, God's will, is always done.

Looking at your present situation, do you feel entangled in the weeds of life, captured, enslaved in stench, and unable to move forward or backward? In what whale belly are you trapped? Did you already know the best decision yet choose to do something different anyway, regardless of the potential consequences? God desires to use each of us, exalt us, and allow our best to manifest for His glory, but how can this happen if we are not completely honest with ourselves or follow His directions? If you cannot trust yourself, how can God trust you? The truth is, He already knows this. We're the ones who usually end up kidding ourselves.

The instructions you receive from God are a set-up, and the foundation for something much bigger than your imagination can handle at the time. Listening, obeying, and following His instructions even if they do not make sense at the time require faith, and faith is necessary for successfully overcoming adversity. Accept your assignment.

3. Stand on the words He gives you.

When God gives you a verse, stand on those words, believe them, and take them as fact. Although His words may appear out of place at that moment, when He speaks to you, believe them. Your spirit knows. If He gives you a word that seems insignificant or opposes your current views or circumstance yet refuses to go away, embrace it and know that He gave it to you for a reason. Abiding in it works in your favor. When God gives you a verse, stand on these words.

The 23rd Psalm was the verse given to me. From a child, I have heard this verse all my life. It was one we all had to memorize and repeat during Sunday school. However, when it was re-implanted into my psyche before another bottom dropped out, it took on a completely different meaning; it wasn't just a cute little Bible verse I had to recite; I was about to live it. In fact, I had no clue of the coming attractions that would again shatter my flimsy veil of security and the world as I knew it. But for that moment, and for whatever reason, I could not get this verse out of my head. It was the calm before the storm.

When the Lord spoke this verse to me, I sat in a parking lot at 4:50 a.m., waiting for my gym to open. I had no idea why that particular verse stuck so firmly in my mind, nor could I begin to imagine the impending danger which lay before me. After receiving this word, I started breaking down every sentence over the next few days. I began dissecting the words and looking at how they applied to my life. I then received instructions to repeat, memorize, and internalize each verse. I thought this strange, but I complied; however, once the storm on the horizon became a reality, the 23rd Psalm was my lifeline to God. Its words meant everything that I wanted to hear.

My life hung by a thread, and this verse kept me alive and forced me to strengthen my faith. It was the umbilical cord that connected me to God. I could finally identify with the realness of those words, not as just a Bible verse, but from a perspective that made them come alive. To this day, I have never looked at the 23rd Psalm the same. Stand on the word of God.

4. See the event or adversity in your life for what it is doing for you, not to you.
When flying on an airplane and experiencing severe turbulence, it becomes difficult to look at what the event is doing for us. All we want is for the episode to be over and get back on solid ground. Being a former flight attendant, I have certainly experienced my share of turbulent flights. I witnessed serving carts thrown around like toys, luggage binds popping open, and passengers slammed against the ceiling, which in some instances made the entire event quite scary. When experiencing this type of turbulence, in almost every case, except for the occasional 'ahhhs' and 'ooohs,' passengers usually get extremely quiet when the bottom drops out. Why?

Because many find themselves evaluating or re-evaluating their lives, they think about getting back on the ground, being with their families, or getting in touch with their spiritual side; in reality, they contemplate the appreciation of life differently. Navigating life's turbulence can be a lot like that too. When faced with turbulent situations where life seems out of control, once the initial shock subsides, many of us also become quiet and reflective. Our goal then becomes to find a place to seek shelter from the buffeting and uncontrollable winds that uproot our security or make us feel as though we lack control. Why? Because we realize, just as you are a passenger riding with an out-of-control driver, you begin to understand that you are not the one in control after all.

When life seems beyond our comprehension, we often become frightened. Without anyone to turn to, we can find ourselves overwhelmed and even depressed. We can begin relying on drugs, alcohol, or anything that momentarily makes us feel better. We may even temporarily forsake God in the process. What we really seek is a coping mechanism, anything that takes the sting out of the situation or, at least, the edge off. The truth is, these temporary measures only mask the pain, not get rid of it entirely.

Once we come back from our temporary solution and face reality, the problems remain. So, is that the right choice? Facing our turbulence from a different perspective allows us to see God's presence in our lives. Proverbs 3:12 states, "For whom the LORD loveth he correcteth; even as a father the son in whom he delighteth." However, who within himself wishes to be corrected? No one.

Having the opportunity to choose our form of correction, would we? If so, would we choose severe turbulence? The belly of a whale, a long-term stay in the emptiness of Noah's ark, or a lion's den? Probably none of these. That is why these challenges were chosen, especially for them, just as ours is for us. When you look at the challenges our biblical lookalikes faced and compare them to what you may be going through, you may find some similarities.

What is your version of Daniel's lion's den? Is it a bunch of cut-throat conniving business partners or greed-filled family members wanting to take your possessions? Being in a lion's den is more than just a story from an old book. It is more than literal and could hold metaphorical truths. It may be currently happening to you or someone on a job, an innocent person in a prison cell, or even a pastor in their own church.

We should remember God does not place adversity in our lives to harm us but prepares us for another phase or level of life. Make no mistake, His method for doing so would not be our choice. Yet, in the end, as we grow, we are much better for having had the experience. Again, like turbulence buffeting an airplane, it may appear as though little is happening inside us, but rest assured, on that airplane, a great deal of change is taking place among the passengers, as it is inside you. Your responsibility is to seek God and find the blessing in your situation instead of merely focusing on the pain, discomfort, and inconvenience it may be causing.

5. Don't be surprised by the lie. Lies have no boundaries.

Anyone who has ever suffered from the effects of a lie can surely understand its far-reaching powers. One lie can wreak havoc on individuals for a lifetime. Their collateral damage has destroyed many relationships, marriages, businesses, and lives. Lies sometimes come across as simple and harmless, you know, like the ones spoken by a friend or colleague, followed by, "Oh, I was just kidding," when in reality, they were merely truths cloaked in clever jokes. Or the so-called little white lie told when someone doesn't want to make another person feel uncomfortable. "Honey, how does this dress look?" "It looks great, honey," is the response when it may not look good at all in reality.

Then there are the blatant, uncloaked, and truly hurtful lies that are painful, highly visible, and make no pretense, while others lie just beneath the surface, mixed with just enough truth to make them believable. They are damning, hurtful, and inflict irreparable damage that ripples through every facet of life. When enough of these partial half-truth lies become stitched together, they create a perception that creates doubt in the minds of those exposed to them. I have suffered from the devastating impact of these types of lies on multiple occasions. Let me tell you; it is not for the faint of heart.

We've all heard the expression of being innocent until proven guilty; however, in many circles, such as the ones I experienced, you are guilty until you prove yourself innocent. The fact is, although you can be completely innocent, you may not be treated like it. You may also be surprised by people you believe to be your friends, who will distance themselves from you during such times. In these instances, your entire career, livelihood, reputation, and character could all be on the line.

A person who practices the art of lying is called a liar. According to the Bible, Satan is the father of lies, and just as we have a heavenly father whom we pattern our lives after, so do individuals used by Satan. People who practice lying are very aware of the devastating power of their craft. Conversely, this is why they do it; to steal, manipulate, take from others, and ultimately destroy. "The thief cometh not, but for to steal, and to kill, and to destroy: I am come that they might have life and that they might have it more abundantly." John 10:10.

If you are experiencing loss brought about as a result of lies, false witness, or deception of any type, know that ultimately, God has a plan for you that the enemy is hell-bent on keeping you from accomplishing. When our Heavenly Father calls us for a greater purpose, the enemy already knows the plan before we do. He desires to derail any possibility of you completing God's plan before you even understand your role in it.

When thinking of the plan or purpose, I think of *The Terminator* movie, which premiered in 1984, starring Arnold Schwarzenegger. Schwarzenegger plays the role of a robot cyborg sent from the future on a mission to go back in time to protect a mother-to-be, Sarah Connor. Sarah's role was to bear a son who would save humanity from being dominated by machines one day. On the other hand, another cyborg from the machines is sent back in time with another mission; to destroy Sara Connor, preventing her from having the son who would ultimately save humanity. Sound familiar?

This movie's plot sounds painfully similar to the struggles of good and evil related to man on this Earth. Although a hard-fought battle ensued and good ultimately triumphed, just think, if this mother and her unborn child were significant enough to warrant a protector from the future to save her, how important are each of us in the fulfillment of God's plan? The problem is our limited understanding of our own destiny; we do not know or have enough insight into the entire plan; only God and Satan do, and Satan will stop at nothing to see that you never accomplish your purpose.

So, as you face your current circumstances, whatever they may be, try and envision your long-term future. Again, avoid looking at what the event is doing to you rather than for you. Know that God is protecting you, covering you, and He has your back, whether it feels like it or not, and He is recalibrating your entire life. Again, avoid looking at what the event is doing to you rather than for you.

Know that the God providing your favor, grace, and mercy, is still in control. If he had wanted you dead, you would be gone by now. He also knows the power of a lie, and the biggest lie the enemy wants you to believe is that you do not matter. He also wants you to believe that God doesn't care about you, you have no purpose, and everyone would be better off if you were not here. Do not believe it. Once you buy into that lie, you are letting him win.

6. Allow yourself to be vulnerable.
When facing challenges, everyone puts on a different face in front of others to hide their pain. I remember an old T.V. commercial for a deodorant that stated, "Never let them see you sweat." In public, most of us follow that rule. But what happens once we get home, the doors close, and we are alone? Does that rule still apply?

If we are truthful, once the enormity of our situation begins to take its toll, even the most faithful individuals can break down under pressure. Feelings of anger at the situation and even others close to you may emerge. Feelings of guilt for having let yourself and others down may appear. Feelings of uncertainty; the "What's gonna happen now?" questions that continually flood your mind make rational thinking difficult. If left unchecked, these thoughts could consume you.

Regardless of who you are, when the pressures of life become unbearable, our minds, bodies, and spirits can collapse under the weight of the stress. It is then when you must humble your mind, thoughts, attitude, and yourself. Allow yourself to be vulnerable to God's mercy and grace. It is then when you give up your way and allow Him to guide you. I Peter 5:6-7. states, "Therefore humble yourselves under the mighty hand of God, that He may exalt you in due time, casting all your cares upon Him, for He cares for you."

We live in a society where it's not 'cool' to appear weak. Believe me, when I say I felt that way myself. As an ex-superhero, I couldn't appear weak. The truth is that humility and weakness are two entirely different things. It takes a great deal of strength to be humble. And although you may humble yourself beyond any point you believe possible, perfection is not the endgame. No one will ever be perfect. None of us can be. We will still have faults, unclean thoughts, make decisions that may not be in our best interest, and fall short of the glory of God. However, they will become less frequent and will not wear our former mindset like a coat of arrogance armor. Remember, you will never get it 100% right, so don't add to the already unbearable pressure that only subsides after the adversity runs its course. How long will this take? Who knows? It ends when its time is up.

It goes back to the statement we've all heard before, "Doing the same thing over again and expecting a different result is a form of insanity. God is trying to get you to stop that insanity. "God says to humble yourselves under his mighty hand, and He will exalt you in due time, meaning, letting go of your old way of thinking and taking on the thought process He has for you. Once you adopt a new mindset, the Lord will restore and place you where He wants you to be. If you were left to your previous nature, your success would all be about you and not Him.

What has brought more meaning to my life than anything I could have imagined is the ability to give up the competitive striving, all the thinking that the world rewards in exchange for the reprogramming and the contentment the Lord rewards. His program and plan for my life are much more rewarding than mine. My investment was humility, trust, and faith in exchange for igniting outstanding breakthroughs and results.

7. Exercise faith through these steps.
Know that exercising faith is like going to the gym. You don't get massive results and grow stronger overnight; it takes time, effort, and commitment. It is the same with faith. Believing in the impossible every day develops your faith. It's blind faith, radical faith, undying faith that turns dreams into reality. Trusting God when the chips are down, after being rejected by the banks, after

being fired and getting no interviews or offers, all require day-in, day-out, workout faith.

What's funny is those who have attained high degrees of success give credit to themselves. It was "I Incorporated," who depended on myself to get things done and make them happen.

Letting go and humbling ourselves to the unseen takes a great deal of blind faith; exercising this type of belief makes us uncomfortable. It is an act we are not accustomed to. That is what God desires of us. The problem is, His way is in opposition to what man believes, but is necessary for you to achieve the fullness of what He wants for you.

Here are ten steps that will assist you in embracing humility and growing your faith.

1. Pray to God in truth and spirit. He already knows what your deal is, so come clean, be honest, and be correct. Your attempt is not to con God by hiding behind half-truths and lying by omission. You cannot get away with it. God already knows the best and worst of you.

2. Allow the event to reveal your true friends and confidants. True friends and confidants become much more difficult to find during stressful and adverse times.

3. Surround yourself with a small group of prayer warriors and people who care about you and are willing to support you through your crises.

4. Keep a steady routine. Focus your energy on journaling, reading, doing something physical, or finding a new hobby. Immerse yourself in educational or volunteer projects so the event doesn't consume you. The expression "The idle mind is the devil's playground;" is never more accurate.
Allow them to provide a mechanism for insight and growth.

5. Always put God first. Do not forsake Him, even if you sometimes feel like it. You must see that He is still with you, and you are not alone. Exercise a measure of hope by taking the event day by day.

6. Know that your emotions are natural and will run the gamut. You may wake up feeling wonderful and full of spirit; however, you could become angry, carnal, or even depressed before lunch. Know that until you regain your focus and balance, these feelings may be possible.

7. Create a "What Is This Event Doing for Me" list. Although challenging, look for the positive in what you are experiencing. God wants you to see that He is pressing you for a reason. He is attempting to get your attention. In fact, He may have been doing so for quite a while; however, this time, you may be listening. Go back to the previous section of this book and review the poem 'Weights.' Realize that the weight placed on you makes you more powerful. Although you may feel punished now, you will understand the purpose of this challenge at some point.

8. During this time, expand yourself as much as possible. Get bigger and increase your knowledge on various subjects. See yourself and your offerings differently. Understand and embrace your current value. Your loss is not what makes you, you. It's what is on the inside of yourself that is your brilliance. Who knows, perhaps a day will come when you must witness someone experiencing some of the same challenges you have. You may never know the impact your story could have on someone's life.

9. Seek God's will for your life. Petition Him to reveal His plan for your purpose and your life. Remember, God has the master plan. He shapes and crafts us from the womb. He already knew what we would accomplish before we did, so seek Him. Also, keep in mind that God's timing is not ours. If you do not receive an answer right away, that's okay; remain patient, and He will reveal it to you in time. When experiencing painful events, it seems as if they will last forever, and God has forsaken us.

When Jesus was being crucified and hanging on the cross, even though He was the son of God, it did not diminish the time He had to suffer on the cross before he died. Again,

God's timing is not ours. So, as you hang on your cross of adversity, what may seem like an eternity to you, may only be a few seconds to God. Know that He has not forsaken you.

10. Trust God. One of the toughest challenges so-called self-made people have is their inability to trust someone or something spiritual over themselves. Again, we're used to the 'me principle.' We are used to getting it done ourselves, so why wait on anyone else. It sort of goes against the grain of who we are; however, when it comes to God, He wants us to trust Him so that He can trust us.

Finally, thank you for taking time from your life to read this book. Again, I hope you realize that you are not alone throughout your struggle or whatever challenges you may face. Others have gone before you, and those yet to follow will face unspeakable adversity, but as always, it does not last forever.

It is also my desire that through these words, you find hope and encouragement for facing each day, for managing your situation, and your healing. I pray the Lord keeps and protects you and your family. May He provide mercy, favor, and grace as you continue along your journey.

Thank you for sharing these precious minutes of your life with me.

All the best.

Steven LeMons

*"If you enjoyed reading The Incredible Journey Of a Life, please leave a review on **www.stevenlemons.com** or **Amazon**. I read every one of your reviews and comments. Your words help new readers discover my book. Oh, and don't forget to visit my other website at **www.thejouneyoflife.me** or email me at **info@thejourneyoflife.me** and please recommend this book to a friend."*

Thank you

About the Author

Steven LeMons is a nationally recognized inspirational keynote speaker, professional development facilitator, cancer survivor, and author. His experiences and travels have taken him to 14 countries and 49 states. He is one of the most dynamic and  exciting speakers at corporate events and college on campuses. Steven's presentations are content-rich and masterfully presented. His messages are captivating, sometimes explosive, always inspiring, provocatively engaging, tastefully humorous, and leave audiences with unforgettable calls to action.

Steven has held key leadership positions as national training director, national training manager, general manager, director of corporate development, television host, and video segment producer. Having served in both the United States Army and Air Force Reserve combined with his content development skills, Steven has created a long list of impressive leadership training, inspirational content, and video segments for thousands of students, administrators, directors, sales, and management professionals.

Steven's hobbies and activities are public speaking, writing, instructional design, strength training, glider flying, music, and spending time with family and close friends.

Acknowledgments

To write acknowledgments recognizing everyone who influenced this book seems unfair in one way or another. However, I will feebly attempt to do so. Although years in its creation, countless individuals crossed my path, touched my heart, warmed my soul, encouraged me, and even inspired me to complete this project.

There are names and people I do remember, and even though there are those I cannot recall, it does not diminish their contribution to my life and this project. Whether my inspiration resulted from the excruciating pain and the adverse emotions experienced from a job firing, or the encouraging and thoughtful suggestions shared during a time of uncertainty from a friend, I cannot deny either's involvement; each is as important as the other.

Over the years, what I find interesting is that whenever I begin a new venture, whether a job, personal project, or any life transition, there are always strategically placed people who enter my life. Whether they played large or small roles, each was equally significant in the overall scheme. Although we never knew how long time would allow us to interact, it was the importance of the lesson and the wisdom gained that made our time together meaningful.

There are also those I do not know personally or have not met face-to-face, but in some way, they commanded my attention and motivated or inspired me to action. Those whom I have watched or listened to through video, a television or radio message, sermon, speech, or even through YouTube, I am eternally grateful for your work and appreciate its impact on my life.

Finally, to everyone who directly or indirectly contributed to this project, thank you for sharing your insight, thoughts, and a portion of yourself with me. I am eternally grateful to be blessed through your connection.

First, I thank God for loving my family and me and sustaining and keeping us when we could not sustain or keep ourselves. Thank you for knowing the outcome when I didn't have faith to know you were always in control. You are the light of my life, and through my successes and shortcomings, this book is about my life and the relationship I grew to have with You.

To my mother, Mrs. Cora Lemons-Wilson. Thank you for making the ultimate sacrifice for myself and my brothers and for introducing us to the guiding light that would be with each of us throughout our lives. I love you.

Tony, Lanier, and Cory, thank each of you for being there for me and for your kind and encouraging words. I am grateful for the times when each of you had a better opinion of me than I had of myself. Thank you for allowing me to understand what the word 'brother' means.

Alicia, the road was long with many lessons learned and scars to prove it. Always wishing you the best.

Nancy LeMons, your friendship, and belief have been invaluable. I appreciate your support.

Mr. Morris Ashmon, although you are gone, you are certainly not forgotten. I miss you, brother.

Ms. Betty Harper, thank you for your patience in sharing with me a piece of carbon that, over time, has become the largest diamond I could ever imagine. I will never forget your contribution.

Randall Reed, it was a 'World Class' pleasure and opportunity to learn and work with you.

Mr. A.J. Guanella, you are a wonderful man.

Ms. Diane Harris, you will always have a friend in me.

Former Lt. Governor of Colorado, Joe Rogers, our talks gave me hope and encouragement through some of my darkest hours.

Michael and Carvetta Williams, your love and support have truly been a blessing over the years.

Paul D. Cummings, thanks for putting the burr in my saddle. It was a lesson at the fencepost I needed.

Pastors T.D. Jakes, Tony Evans, Chuck Swindoll, and Dr. Charles Stanley, your ministries have changed my life in ways you will never know.

Michael Saunders, thank you for always being there for me when there was no one else. I will always value our friendship.

Cherilynn Bates, I love you for seeing the love in me I always knew existed, but no one else could see. Thank you.

Dr. Tahita Fulkerson, your encouragement and value in me when I lost track of who I was has been invaluable.

Bill McMullen, my true friend, confidant, supporter, and brother. Thank you for believing in my work.

Dr. Scott & Kathy Robinson, thank you both for sharing your invaluable encouragement when I needed it most.

Dr. Jim & Terri Schrantz, thank you for inviting me on the journey.

Donye Smith and Sierra Roundtree, may you both rest in eternal peace.

And to the countless unnamed individuals who crossed my path and touched my life. Whether the experience was perceived as positive or unpleasant, thank you for my opportunity for growth through encountering you. May God continue to grant each of you grace, mercy, and favor throughout your lives.

To all the incredible photographers who must be recognized for contributing their beautiful images to this project, thank you and the Unsplash team.

Photography Acknowledgements

Special thanks to **Fernand De Canne** *on Unsplash for the front cover photo*
Johnannes Plenio *on Unsplash for the back cover photo*
Photo by Mario Dobelmann on Unsplash
Photo by Greg Rakozy on Unsplash
Photo by Laura Vinck on Unsplash
Photo by Lucas Clarysse on Unsplash
Photo by Marek Piwnicki on Unsplash
Photo by Ian Espinosa on Unsplash
Photo by Zygimantas Dukauskas on Unsplash
Photo by Rachel Coyne on Unsplash
Photo by Debby Hudson on Unsplash
Photo by Alex Iby on Unsplash
Photo by Cristian Newman on Unsplash
Photo by Baptiste Gousset on Unsplash
Photo by Gaelle Marcel-Azod on Unsplash
Photo by Philipp Berndt on Unsplash
Photo by Evie S. on Unsplash
Photo by Sharon McCutcheon on Unsplash
Photo by Anne Edgar on Unsplash
Photo by Alexander Krivitskiy on Unsplash
Photo by Emilio Garcia
Photo by Yousef Alfuhigi-Yuu on Unsplash